THE 100 BEST BRITISH GHOST STORIES

THE 100 BEST BRITISH GHOST STORIES

Ghosts, Poltergeists, Boggarts & Black Dogs from the Oral Tradition

selected and edited by
Gillian Bennett

AMBERLEY

For family and friends

Front cover: The ruined keep of Longtown Castle, Herefordshire
Longtown lies in a valley at the foot of the Black Mountains. It was to Longtown that a Herefordshire man was travelling when he encountered the ghost of 'T. H.' See 'The Guide to the Black Mountains', story no. 76. Photograph by Andrew F. Bennett.

Back cover: Entrance to Castle Rising Castle, Norfolk
See 'The Fiddler and his Dog', story no. 41. Photograph by Andrew F. Bennett.

First published 2012

Amberley Publishing
The Hill, Stroud
Gloucestershire, GL5 4EP

www.amberleybooks.com

British Library Cataloguing in Publication Data.
A catalogue record for this book is available from the British Library.

ISBN 978 1 4456 0694 1

Typesetting and Origination by Amberley Publishing.
Printed in Great Britain.

Contents

PART 2: THE EIGHTEENTH CENTURY

PART 3: THE NINETEENTH CENTURY

Acknowledgement

Much of the work for this book has been done by my husband Andrew. He has discussed research and production issues with me, sourced texts and images, surfed the internet, discovered the location of way-out places, driven me to them guided by his own internal SatNav, and taken all the photographs that illustrate this book. What a star!

Preface

The stories in this volume are drawn from my own collection, which was built up over the last thirty years or so and spans four centuries of storytelling.

The oldest stories were first told in the middle years of the seventeenth century, when the existence or non-existence of ghosts was hotly debated by the religious and intellectual establishment; the most recent were told to me personally in the early 1980s when I was collecting material for what was to be my first book, *Traditions of Belief*. In the centuries between, interest in ghosts and ghost stories fluctuated. During the eighteenth century, educated opinion was firmly opposed to belief in ghosts, and the telling of ghost stories was regarded as an entertainment fit only for women and children. However, interest revived in the nineteenth century when, under the influence of evolutionary theory, leading members of the Folklore Society (established 1878) collected folk tales and legends as evidence of the survival of earlier stages of culture.

In all that time, certain features of ghost belief have remained constant. By and large, in our culture ghosts are thought to be immaterial spirits appearing or operating in material form; they may be the essence of a living creature (usually human but sometimes animal) or, more commonly, the spiritual residue of a dead or dying person. They may be malign or benign: if malign, their sole aim seems to be to harass those to whom they appear; if benign, their purposes are ordinary human ones – they may be motivated by a desire for justice or revenge, for example, or they may come out of love for their family, or to see order and decency restored to human behaviour, or to bring messages from the other world. The stories in this book all rely on these assumptions. Many are legends, traditional stories illustrative of local folklore; others are experience stories which, whilst claiming to be individual and personal, spring from the same cultural tradition.

These stories rightly belong to an oral not a literary tradition, though of course in Britain today nothing can be uniquely oral. Stories in particular have the habit of slipping from word-of-mouth to print to screen to cyberspace and back again more or less randomly, and cyberspace has replaced face-to-face communication as the primary medium of social interaction for a surprising number of people. However, I think we can still use the term 'oral' meaningfully. Speaking for myself, when I talk of 'ghost stories from the oral tradition' I mean stories which will, whatever their traceable history, at some formative time have been passed by word of mouth from tellers to hearers sharing the same cultural traditions.

Times and Places

Without exception, the stories in this book are located in a named town, building, house, moor, lake, or road. In about twenty this reference is sketchy – 'not far from Cirencester'; 'one of the mountainous districts of Monmouthshire, called Blaenau Gwent' (story no. 27); 'certain spots on Dartmoor' (story no. 70) – but in the majority of cases the locations are quite specific; they can be found on a map and visited. In trips to Lancashire, the Welsh Borders, Cornwall and Devon, London, Yorkshire and Norfolk, my husband Andrew and I were able to stand at the exact spot mentioned in about half of these locations. If time had allowed, we could probably have taken photographs in most of the remainder.

Speaking for myself, I have found it very interesting and enlightening to visit these scenes. Not only has it made the stories come alive, but it has also let me see why people have found it easy to believe them. In so many cases there is something distinctive about the location – something unpleasant, special or discordant. Writing in 1866, William Henderson observed that

> The universal voice of mankind has ever pointed out certain places as the borderland between the material and the spiritual world ... In general, places which once were closely connected with man, but are now deserted by him, are thus distinguished in the popular mind, rather than those which have always been barren and desolate.

I don't think this is entirely correct. The fact that many of these places have been deserted by humankind is relevant, I am sure, but I think it is equally significant that the place itself commands attention in some way.

Exceptional places have been the focus of many a local legend: tales of giants who move mountains, devils who transplant churches or twist the steeple, or lovers who leap to their deaths over deep ravines have proliferated. But a search for a 'why so' explanation is not the only natural human response. The sense of wonder or unease can, I think, just as easily be acknowledged by attributing some supernatural force or uncanny event to it. Many of the locations we visited have just such an atmosphere, created by the strangeness of their natural or man-made features. The canal-bridge where the 'Man-Monkey' jumped on the horse of a Shropshire carrier and scared him half to death (story no. 53), for example, is no ordinary bridge. The height of two or three double-decker buses, Thomas Telford's bridge spans a deep cutting through which the narrow canal blackly slinks. Its height makes it necessary for the bridge to be braced with a secondary arch, giving the impression of a lower road passing beneath the road one is travelling on; the reflections of this double arch in the black water of the canal further adds to the dissonance of the scene. Likewise, the church of St Etheldreda at Hyssington, where the Roaring Bull of Bagbury was finally conquered by twelve pious and patient men (story no. 60), stands a good mile from the village itself and is dominated by ancient earthworks which tower over the church. 'Boggart Hole Clough' (story no. 37), too, is an unexpected sort of place – no ordinary urban park. Did the name of this wild and dark ravine come before the legend or the legend before the name?

It is interesting, too, to discover that these local (or localised) legends are cherished by the community, and find a place in any exhibition of local history in churches as well as museums. At Hyssington, for example, someone has painted a picture of the exorcism of the Roaring Bull and hung it on the wall of the south aisle near the entrance to the church; and at Talland the extensive and informed display of local events from medieval times onwards, not only has a board on which the exploits of Parson Dodge are recorded, but a ring-binder of local legends containing, among other things, a version of 'Parson Dodge and the Spectral Coach' (story no. 33) other than the familiar version found in Robert Hunt's *Popular Romances of the West of England* – somebody has done their research!

But a good story travels, so many of the stories in this book are what folklorists call 'migratory legends' – that is, they are stories which have been told in many places, each time as new, local and possibly 'true' events. A story about a flitting boggart, for example, may be told pretty much simultaneously in Lancashire and in Lincolnshire and will be decked out with all sorts of local knowledge and provenance (see stories no. 37 and 86). Similarly, a tale about a ghost bringing help to a dying man will be told as personal experience in St Petersburg and in Shropshire (see stories no. 80 and 91), though at each time and in each place the event seems to be very real and very local.

Story Selection and Presentation

It is partly for this reason that I have preferred not to arrange the stories in the customary way by region, but to group them chronologically and pick up on the way ghost-lore changes over time. Though this book does not claim to be a history of ghosts I have tried to choose stories that are typical of the age in which they were told. There are four main sections, presenting stories from the seventeenth, eighteenth, nineteenth and twentieth centuries. Each section is prefaced with an introduction which sets the stories in their context; and each story has a headnote which aims to contextualise them further by adding information about such things as the publication history of the story, the lives of the featured characters, or the place where the events are supposed to have occurred.

For historical reasons and reasons of authenticity, I have chosen to leave the stories in their original form and interfered as little as possible with stylistic features, punctuation and spelling. Again, this is not the usual practice, but I do not think readers will have any difficulty with older prose styles. Indeed, I hope they will appreciate them and enjoy the changing narrative styles as they move from the elaborate stories of seventeenth century to the simple – almost naïve – stories with which I end.

Finally, the bulk of these stories are in prose, but so that we don't forget that there are some striking ghost stories in the ballad tradition, I have begun and ended with a ballad – the touching fragment 'The Unquiet Grave' at the beginning of the volume and the comic story of 'Old Grindrod's Ghost' at the end.

Gillian Bennett
Betws-y-Coed

Bookend 1

1
The Unquiet Grave
(Child Ballad no. 78)

The wind doth blow today, my love,
And gently drops the rain.
I've never had but one true love,
In cold grave she was lain.

I'll do as much for my true love,
As any young man may,
I'll sit and mourn upon her grave,
For twelve months and a day.

When twelve months and a day was passed,
The dead began to speak,
Oh who sits weeping on my grave
And will not let me sleep?

'Tis I, my love, sits on your grave
And will not let you sleep;
For I crave one kiss of your clay-cold lips
And that is all I seek.

You crave one kiss of my clay-cold lips
But my breath smells earthy strong,
And if you have one kiss of my cold clay lips,
Your days will not be long.

'Tis down in yonder garden green
Where we were wont to walk,
The fairest flower that e'er was seen
Is withered to a stalk.

The stalk is withered dry, my love
So will our hearts decay;
So make yourself content, my love
Till God calls you away.

– Kinsley, ed., *The Oxford Book of Ballads*, p. 96.

PART 1

The Seventeenth Century

Introduction

Anyone interested in the history of ghost beliefs in Britain will find the period from 1530 to the end of the seventeenth century particularly interesting, spanning as it does two movements which put the existence and nature of ghosts in the forefront of debate.

The first of these movements was the Reformation. At no time was the answer to the question of whether there were such things as ghosts more obviously a gateway to understanding someone else's worldview.

One of the bones of contention was the concept of Purgatory. Protestant divines insisted there was no such place; at death the soul went straight to Heaven or straight to Hell. Catholics, on the other hand, championed the old concept of a three-dimensional afterlife consisting of Heaven, Hell and Purgatory. Both Catholics and Protestants agreed that the souls of bad people would not be allowed to escape from Hell and the souls of good people would not wish to leave Heaven. The only place restless spirits could be coming from was therefore Purgatory, which was conceived of as a sort of holding pen where souls could be purged of sin. It followed that if there was no Purgatory, there could be no ghosts; but if ghosts could be proved to exist, the existence of Purgatory was confirmed. Hence, the competing religious/philosophical positions were debated very largely through treatises about supernatural occurrences and collections of stories about ghosts.

The Catholic argument was simple and, or so it appeared, incontrovertible – the Bible, tradition and experience all gave substantial evidence of the existence of ghosts. To counter these arguments Protestant writers began by first discrediting stories of ghostly experiences as delusions, mistakes, deceit, or deliberate lies. Where no 'natural' explanation could be found, they argued that such apparitions must either be enchantments of the devil or good angels sent by God on a special mission. This is Shakespeare's Hamlet's dilemma when he encounters the ghost of his father: 'Angels and ministers of grace defend us!' he exclaims. 'Be thou a spirit of health or goblin damned/Bring with thee airs from Heaven or blasts from Hell/Be thy intents wicked or charitable, I'll speak with thee ...'

By the mid-seventeenth century a new debate had arisen. The arrival of the scientific viewpoint – or as it was known then, the 'mechanical philosophy' – was greeted with horror by many pious people who regarded it as outright atheism. Again the battle was fought in part through the dissemination of legends and personal stories about divine intervention and supernatural happenings. It was in this climate that such as Joseph Glanvil (1636–80), Richard Baxter (1615–91), Richard Bovet (born *c.* 1641) and George Sinclair (d. 1696) collected and published their 'relations' of ghosts and strange happenings in the latter part of the century to give evidence of divine operations in the mundane world. Eight of the stories below come from one or other of these sources.

The interests of John Aubrey (1626–97), another great collector of supernatural stories whose narratives feature in the selection that follows, were rather different. A man of almost unlimited curiosity – a pioneer archaeologist and antiquarian who recorded numerous megaliths and field monuments in southern England – his name is now associated with both Avebury and the 'Aubrey holes' at Stonehenge. His *Miscellanies on Various Subjects* of 1696 is a lively collection of rumours, gossip, legends and personal experiences. Six of the stories below come from Aubrey. Other sources are contemporary accounts, later folklore collections and regional histories.

Despite the differences between these writers, there were many similarities. Seventeenth-century ghost stories shared a number of characteristics, as follows:

- (i) Ghosts were seen as either benign or malign, purposeful or purposeless.
- (ii) At the 'malign' end of the spectrum were poltergeists, interpreted either as evil spirits ('demons' or 'daemons' in contemporary terminology) or as instances of witchcraft. Malign spirits might also assault the living, strip garments and bedclothes off their victims while they slept, or try to get into bed with them.
- (iii) Benign ghosts were expected to return to address wrongs, warn of danger, reveal secrets, or cure sickness.
- (iv) Purposeful ghosts returned to demand proper burial, to ensure their dying wishes had been observed, to testify to the existence of God and the Devil or to provide evidence of murder (usually their own).
- (v) Ghosts also returned as the result of an unholy pact to test the reality of an afterlife; in this case they nearly always announced their own damnation.

(vi) Ghosts appeared as wraiths at the time of the death of the body. Also, since, at this time, a ghost was not necessarily the appearance of a dead – or even dying – person, they might appear to those they loved in times of danger or distress (as John Donne's wife did; see story no. 17), or (as in the case of Baxter's Colonel Bowen; see story no. 4) their ugly soul might leave their still-living body and show itself in its true form to the horror of all who encountered them.

2
An Apparition in Cirencester

This is possibly the shortest and most intriguing ghost story ever recorded.

Anno 1670, not far from Cirencester, was an apparition: being demanded, whether a good spirit, or a bad? returned no answer, but disappeared with a curious perfume and a most melodious twang.

– Aubrey, *Miscellanies*, p. 82.

3
Captain Henry Bell Explains How He Found Time to Translate the Works of Martin Luther

This story is the preface to Bell's translation of The Table Talk of Martin Luther, *1650. My quotation is of the central part of the narrative. Previously Bell has explained that whilst he was in Germany on state business during the reign of James I, 'I did hear and understand in all places, great bewailing and lamentation made by reason of the destroying and burning of above four-score thousand of Martin Luther's books, entitled "His Last Divine Discourses".' By immense good fortune, however, one of Luther's original books was found buried in the foundations of the house of a German friend, and was sent to Bell in England with the request that it should be translated.*

Whereupon I took the said book before me [Bell continues] and many times began to translate the same, but always I was hindered therein, being called upon about other business: insomuch, that by no possible means I could remain by that work. Then, about six weeks after I had received the said book, it fell out, that I being in bed one night, between twelve and one of the clock, my wife being asleep, myself yet awake, there appeared unto me an ancient man, standing at my bedside, arrayed all in white, having a long and broad white beard hanging down to his girdle steed, who taking me by my right car, spake these words following unto me: 'Sirrah! will not you take time to translate that book which is sent unto you out of Germany? I will shortly provide for you both time and place to do it'; and then he vanished away out of my sight.

Whereupon being much thereby affrighted, I fell into an extreme sweat: insomuch, that my wife awaking, and finding me all over wet, she asked me what I ailed? I told her what I had seen and heard: but I never did heed nor regard visions nor dreams. And so the same fell soon out of my mind.

Then about a fortnight after I had seen that vision, on a Sunday, I went to Whitehall to hear the sermon; after which ended, I returned to my lodging, which was then at King-street, at Westminster, and sitting down to dinner with my wife, two messengers were sent from the whole council-board, with a warrant to carry me to the keeper of the Gatehouse, Westminster, there to be safely kept, until further order from the lords of the council; which was done without showing me any cause at all wherefore I was committed. Upon which said warrant I was kept ten whole years close prisoner, where I spent five years thereof about the translating of the said book; insomuch as I found the words very true which the old man, in the aforesaid vision, did say unto me – 'I will shortly provide for you both place and time to translate it.'

Bell then goes on to describe the translation's reception in England by Archbishop Laud and others, its passage through the House of Commons in 1646, its publication, and his eventual release from prison. The account, he says, was 'Given under my hand the third day of July, 1650'.

– Captain Henry Bell, *Lutheri Posthuma*, Preface.

4
Colonel Bowen Visits His Wife

The events recorded in this famous story supposedly occurred during or just after the English Civil War (1642–51) and were much talked of at the time. There are several contemporaneous accounts, of which the following is the first of two collected by the Shropshire divine, Richard Baxter, and published in 1691. It is dated as 'August 1656'.

In the beginning of the late war, a gentleman of the county, being oppressed by the King's party, took arms under the Earl of Essex, and by his valour obtained good repute in the army, so that in a short time he got the command of lieutenant-colonel. But as soon as the heat of the war was abated, his ease and preferment led him to a careless and sensual life, insomuch that the godly commanders judged him unfit to continue in England, and thereupon sent him to Ireland, where he grew so vain and notional, that he was cashiered the army, and being then at liberty to sin without restraint, he became an absolute Atheist, denying Heaven or hell, God or devil (acknowledging only a power, as the ancient heathens did fate), accounting all temporal pleasures all his expected heaven, so that at last he became hateful, and hating all civil society, and nearest relations.

About December last, he being in Ireland, and his wife (a godly gentlewoman, of good family ...) living in this house in Glamorgan, was very much troubled one night with a great noise, much like the sound of a whirlwind, and a violent beating of the doors or walls, as if the whole house was falling to pieces; and being in her chamber, with most of her family, after praying to the Lord ... she went to bed, and suddenly after, there appeared unto her something like her husband, and asked her whether he should come to bed. She, sitting up, and praying to the Lord, told him he was not her husband, and that he should not. He urged more earnestly: – 'What! Not the husband of thy bosom? What! Not the husband of thy bosom?' Yet had no power to hurt her. And she, together with some godly people, spent that night in prayer, being very often interrupted by this apparition.

The next night, Mr Miles (a godly minister), with four other godly men, came to watch and pray in the house for that night, and so continued in prayer and other duties of religion, without any interruption or noise that night. But the night following, the gentlewoman, with several other godly women, being in the house, the noise of whirlwind began again, with more violence than formerly, and the apparition walked in the chamber, having an insufferable stench, like that of a putrified carcass, filling the room with a thick smoak, smelling like sulphur, darkening the light of the fire and candle, but not quite extinguishing it; sometimes going down the stairs, and coming up again with a fearful noise, disturbing them at their prayers, one while with the sound of words which they could not discern, other while striking them so the next morning their faces were black with smoak, and their bodies swollen with bruises.

Thereupon they left the house, lest they should tempt the Lord by their over-bold staying in such danger, and sent this Atheist the sad news of this apparition; who, coming to England about May last, expressed more love and respect to his wife than formerly; yet telling her, that he could not believe her relation of what she had seen, as having not a power to believe any thing but what himself saw; and yet would not hitherto go to his house to make trial, but probably will e'er long, for that he is naturally of an exceeding rash and desperate spirit.

– Baxter, *The Certainty of the World of Spirits*, pp. 44–54.

5
The Demon of Burton

This story comes from the village of Weobley on the 'black and white' trail, 10 miles south-west of Leominster. There are several Burtons in the vicinity, but it is not possible to identify the farmhouse that features in the story. Ella Leather, who published this account in her Folklore of Herefordshire, *says that details of the poltergeist's 'pranks' were 'preserved in a letter' which she quotes as follows:*

There is a farm in Burton, a village in the parish of Weobley, which Mr William Bridges, a linen draper of London, has in mortgage from one Thomas Tomkyns, a decayed yeoman. This farm was taken in by lease of Mrs Elizabeth Bridges, about Michaelmas, 1669. Soon after this tenant was entered on the farm, some familiar began to act apish pranks by knocking boldly at the door in the dark of the evening, and the like in the early morning, but nobody to be seen. The stools and forms were thrown into disorder, heaps of malt and vetches mingled, loaves of bread laid on the table carried into another room, or hid in tubs covered with cloths; cabbage plants dug up and replanted in various patterns; a half roasted pig demolished except the bones; the milk turned sour with vinegar; some cattle died, and among others a sow leaped and danced in strange postures, and at last fell down dead; a mow of pulse and pease likewise.

After [that] one John Jones, a valiant Welshman, undertook to keep watch with a sword, a mastiff dog, and a lantern. He had not long lain on the bed when he heard a knocking at the door, and ... many cats came into his chamber, broke the windows, and made a hideous noise. The mastiff howled, the candle went out, the Welshman fell into a cold sweat, left the sword unused, and with much ado found the door and ran half a mile without looking behind him, protesting next day he would not be another night in the house for a hundred pounds. These particulars I received from an eye witness of unquestionable credit, and you may no more doubt the truth of them than distrust the affection of

Your humble servant
J. A.
Hereford, March 1670.

– Leather, *Folklore of Herefordshire*, pp. 39–40.

6
The Demon of Spraiton

This fantastical poltergeist story is the fourth 'Relation' in Richard Bovet's Pandaemonium; Or The Devil's Cloister, *published in 1684. Only nine original copies of this rare book have been located to date, and little is known about the author, who was probably born in or around the year 1641. The case of the 'Demon of Spraiton' (modern-day Spreyton near Crediton, Devon) was widely discussed contemporaneously. Bovet's account seeks to confirm and clarify these accounts, especially a story previously published in 1683 in a letter from 'T. C. Esquire'. Bovet dates the occurrences to 1682, and says that the events were also 'known to and related by the Reverend Minister of Barnstable, of the vicinity to Spraiton'. Since then, he says, he has received further 'testimonials', which have encouraged him to reprint the story. I have slightly abridged the account as related by Bovet but retained the original spelling and punctuation.*

About the month of November in the year 1682, in the Parish of Spraiton, in the County of Devon, one Francis Fey (Servant to Mr Philip Furze) being in a Field near the dwelling house of his said Master, there appeared unto him, the resemblance of an Aged Gentleman, like his masters Father, with a Pole or Staff in his hand, resembling that he was wont to carry when living, to kill the moles withal: The spectrum approached near the young man, whom you may imagin not a little surprized at the appearance of one that he knew to be dead; but the spectrum bid him not be afraid of him, but tell his Master (who was his Son) that several Legacies which by his Testament he had bequeathed were unpaid, naming Ten Shillings to one and Ten Shillings to another, both which persons he named to the young man, who replyed, that the party he last named was dead, and so it could not be paid to him;

The Ghost answered, He knew that, but it must be paid to the next Relation, whom he also named: The spectrum likewise ordered him to carry Twenty Shillings to a Gentlewoman, Sister to the deceased, living near Totness in the said County, and promised if these things were performed to trouble him no further; but at the same time the spectrum, speaking of his second wife, (who was also dead, called her wicked woman; though the Gentleman who writ the letter knew her, and esteemed her a very good woman: And (having thus related him his mind) the spectrum left the young man; who according to the direction of the Spirit took care to see the small Legacies satisfied, and carryed the Twenty Shillings, that was appointed to be paid the Gentlewoman near Totness, but she utterly refused to receive it; being sent her (as she said) from the Devil: The same night the young man Lodging at her house, the aforesaid spectrum appeared to him again; whereupon the young man challenged his promise, not to trouble him any more, saying, he had performed all according to his appointment, but that the Gentlewoman, his Sister, would not receive the Money: To which the spectrum replied, that was true indeed; but withal directed the young man to ride to Totness, and buy for her a Ring of that value, which the Spirit said she would accept of; which being provided accordingly, she received: Since the performance of which the Ghost, or Apparition of the old Gentleman, hath seemed to be at rest, having never given the young man any further trouble.

But the next day after having delivered the ring, the young man was riding home to his Masters house, accompanyed by a Servant of the Gentlewomans near Totness, and near about the time of their entrance (or a little before they came) into the Parish of Spraiton afore-said, there appeared to be upon the horse behind the young man, the resemblance of the second wife of the old Gentleman, spoken of before. This Demon often threw the young man off his horse, and cast him with such violence to the ground, as was great astonishment, not only to the Gentlewomans Servant (with him) but to divers others, who were spectators of the frightful action, the ground resounding with great noise, by reason of the incredible force, with which he was cast upon it. At his coming into his Masters yard, the horse which he rid, though very poor, & out of case, leaped at one spring 25 foot, to the amazement of all that saw it. Soon after the She-spectre shewed her self to divers in the house (viz.) the aforesaid young man, mistress Thomasin Gidly, Ann Langdon born in that Parish, and a little Child, which by reason of the troublesomeness of the Spirit, they were fain to remove from that house. She appeared sometimes in her own shape, sometimes in forms very horrid, now and then like a monstrous Dog belching out fire, at another time [she] flew out at the window, in the shape of a Horse, carrying with it only one pane of glass, & a small piece of Iron. [...]

When the young man was returning from his Labour, he was taken up by the skirt of his doublet, by this Female Demon, and carried a heighth into the Air: He was soon missed by his Master, and some other Servants that had been at labour with him; and after diligent enquiry, no news could be heard of him, until at length (near half an hour after) he was heard singing, and whistling in a bog, or quagmire, where they found him in a kind of Trance, or extatick fit ... but when he returned again to himself (which was about an hour after) he solemnly protested to them, that the Demon had carried him so high, that his Masters house seemed to him to be but as a Hay-cock; and that during all that time, he was in perfect sense, and prayed to Almighty God not to suffer the Devil to destroy him: and that he was suddenly set down in that Quagmire.

The Workmen found one Shoe on one side of his Masters house, and the other on the other side, and in the morning espied his Perriwig hanging on the top of a Tree: by which it appears he had been carried a considerable heighth, and that what he told them was not a Fiction. [...]

After this, the Spirit continued to molest the young man in a very severe and rugged manner, often handling him with great extremity; and whether it hath yet left its violences to him, or whether the young man be yet alive, I can have no certain account.

I leave the reader to consider of the extraordinary strangeness of the relation.

– Bovet, *Pandaemonium*, pp. 107–13.

7
Dorothy Dingley

This much-anthologised local legend can be found in several nineteenth- and early twentieth-century folklore collections including Sabine Baring-Gould's Cornish Characters and Grand Events, *Robert Hunt's* Popular Romances of the West of England, *and C. S. Gilbert's* An Historical (and Topographical) Survey of the County of Cornwall. *It can also be found in Christina Hole's* Haunted England *and in more recent folklore collections such as Deane and Shaw's* Folklore of Cornwall.

The origin of the legend would appear to be an account entitled 'A Remarkable Passage of an Apparition 1665', now known to be the work of Revd John Ruddle, Vicar of St Mary Magdalene, Launceston, Cornwall. Originally ascribed either to William Bond or Daniel Defoe, it is one of the items in The History of the Life and Adventures of Mr Duncan Campbell *(1720).*

The most familiar version is probably the one Hunt gives in 1865 under the title 'Laying a Ghost'. Hunt ascribes his version to Gilbert. A less familiar version, and probably the most idiosyncratic, is that appearing in William Andrews' Church Treasury *of 1898. It is in an essay on 'Ghost-Layers and Ghost-Laying' by the Revd R. Wilkins Rees, who quotes extensively from an account by the Revd R. A. Hawker of Morwenstow who claims that Ruddle's diary 'fell by chance' into his hands. The story begins as usual with the case of a depressed boy coming to Ruddle's attention (here the parson is called William Rudall), and the boy's confession that he was being haunted. Rudall then goes to see his bishop to get permission to exorcise the ghost and signs a paper swearing him to secrecy. He then goes to the haunted field, puts on a brass ring, draws a pentacle round himself, and plants a twig of rowan in the middle. Going to the south end of the pentacle, he faces due north and waits for the ghost. He addresses her in Syriac, 'the speech which is used, they say, where such ones dwell in thoughts that glide'. He asks her (Dorothy Dinglet, in this account) why her spirit is restless and requests a sign that she is 'a true spirit and not a false fiend'. Dorothy prophesies that 'before next Yule-tide a fearful pestilence [will] lay waste the land, and myriad of souls [will] be loosened from their flesh' (note, the year is 1665, the year the plague struck London). Finally, ghost and parson converse 'with many more words', but it was not lawful 'to set them down', and Rudall goes off to confront the [unnamed] man Dorothy has returned to denounce. Next day he returns, carrying a message of repentance from the sinner who has wronged her, and then 'with certain fixed rites' he dismisses 'that troubled ghost'. Lively though this account is, I suspect it may not be what it claims to be and prefer the version printed below which appears to keep quite closely to the probably more authentic account in* The History of the Life and Adventures of Mr Duncan Campbell. *It comes from a collection of Cornish folklore by Fortescue Hitchins published in 1824.*

The name of the apparition in Hunt and most other sources is given as Dorothy Dingley, but she is also frequently called Dinglet, as in Hawker's account. In Hitchins' account she is Dorothy Durant.

Whoever or whatever the apparition was, the exorcist was certainly real enough – there is a memorial to 'Johanes Ruddle A. M.' in the south aisle of St Mary Magdalene's church, Launceston, showing his death in 1698 at the age of sixty-two. Cambridge University's list of alumni confirms that John Ruddle was indeed Vicar of Launceston and Altarnum, Prebendary of Exeter, and master of the local grammar school.

About 152 years since, a ghost is said to have made its appearance in this parish in a field about half a mile from Botaden or Botathen. In a narrative which is given of this occurence, it is said to have been seen by a son of Mr Bligh aged about sixteen, by his father and mother, and by the reverend John Ruddle, master of the grammar school of Launceston, and one of the prebendaries of Exeter, and vicar of Alternon. The relation given by Mr Ruddle is in substance as follows:

Young Mr Bligh, a lad of bright parts and of no common attainments, became on a sudden pensive, dejected, and melancholy. His friends observing the change without being able to discover the cause, attributed his behaviour to laziness, – an aversion to school, – or some other motive which they suspected he was ashamed to avow. He was, however, induced after some time to inform his brother that in a field through which he passed to and from school, he was invariably met by the apparition of a woman, whom he personally knew when living, and who had been dead about eight years. Ridicule, threats, and persuasions were alike used in vain by the family to induce him to dismiss these absurd ideas. Mr Ruddle was however sent for, to whom the lad ingenuously communicated the time, manner, and frequency of this appearance. It was in a field called Higher Broomfield. The apparition, he said, appeared dressed in female attire, met him two or three times while he passed through the field, glided hastily by him, but never spoke. He had thus been occasionally met about two months before he took any particular notice of it; at length the appearance became more frequent, meeting him both morning and evening, but always in the same field, yet invariably moving out of the path when it came close by him. He often spoke, but could never get any reply. To avoid this unwelcome visitor he forsook the field, and went to school and returned from it through a lane in which place between the quarry-park and nursery it always met him.

Unable to disbelieve the evidence of his senses, or to obtain credit with any of his family, he prevailed upon Mr Ruddle to accompany him to the place. 'I arose,' says this clergyman, 'the next morning and went with him. The field to which he led me I guessed to be about twenty acres, in an open country, and about three furlongs from any house. We went into the field, and had not gone a third part before a spectrum in the shape of a woman, with all the circumstances he had described the day before ... passed by ...

'On 27 July 1665, I went to the haunted field by myself, and walked the breadth of it without any encounter. I then returned, and took the other walk [through the lane], and then the spectre appeared to me, much about the place in which I saw it when the young gentleman was with me. It appeared to move swifter than before ... in so much as I had not time to speak to it as I had determined with myself before hand. The evening of this day the parents, the son and myself being in the chamber where I lay, I proposed to them our going together to the place the next morning. We accordingly met at the stile we had appointed; thence we all four walked into the field together. We had not gone more than half the field before the ghost made its appearance. It then came over the stile just before us, and moved with such rapidity that by the time we had gone six or seven steps, it passed by. I immediately turned my head and ran after it with the young man by my side. We saw it pass over the stile at which we entered, and no farther. I stepped upon the hedge at one place, and the young man at another, but we could discern nothing; whereas I do aver, that the swiftest horse in England could not have conveyed himself out of sight in that short space of time. Two things I observed in this day's appearance; first, a spaniel dog which had followed the company unregarded, barked and ran away, as the spectrum passed by ... Secondly, the motion of the spectrum was not *gradatim* or by steps, or moving of the feet, but by a kind of gliding as children upon ice, or as a boat down a river ... This ocular evidence clearly convinced, but withal strangely affrighted the old gentleman and his wife. They well knew this woman, Dorothy Durant, in her lifetime; were at her burial; and now plainly saw her features in this apparition.

'The next morning being Thursday, I went very early by myself, and walked for about an hour's space in meditation and prayer in the field next adjoining. Soon after five, I stepped over the stile into the haunted field, and had not gone above thirty or forty paces before the ghost appeared at the further stile. I spoke to it in some short sentences, with a loud voice; whereupon it approached, but slowly, and when I came near it moved not. I spoke again, and it answered again in a voice which was neither very audible nor intelligible. I was not the least terrified, therefore I persisted until it spoke again, and gave me satisfaction; but the work could not be finished at this time. Whereupon the same evening, an hour after sunset it met me again, near the same place, and after a few words on each side it quietly vanished, and neither doth appear since, nor ever will more to any man's disturbance. The discourse in the morning lasted about a quarter of an hour.

'These things are true, and I know them to be so, with as much certainty as eyes and ears can give me; and until I can be persuaded that my senses all deceive me ... I must and will assert, that the things in this paper are true.'

– Hitchins, *The History of Cornwall*, pp. 548–51.

8
Five Very Fine and Lovely Women

This is the eighth 'Relation' in Richard Bovet's Pandaemonium *of 1684. He tells his readers that it is an account of 'divers strange Appearances of Spirits in a Noblemans House in the West'. The original spelling and punctuation have been retained.*

About the year 1667, being with some Persons of Honour at the House of a Nobleman in the West Country, which had formerly been a Nunnery: I must confess I had often heard the Servants, and others that inhabited, or lodged there, speak much of the noises, stirs, and Apparitions that frequently disturbed the House, but had at that time no apprehensions of it; for the House being full of Strangers, the Noblemans Steward, Mr C. lay with me in a fine Wainscot Room, called my Ladies Chamber; we went to our Lodging pretty early, and having a good fire in the Room, we spent some time in reading, in which he much delighted: then having got into Bed, and put out the Candles, we observed the Room to be very light, by the brightness of the Moon, so that a Wager was laid between us, that it was possible to read written hand by that light upon the Bed where we lay; accordingly I drew out of my Pocket a Manuscript, which he read distinctly in the place where he lay: We had scarce made an end of discoursing about that affair, when I saw (my face being towards the door, which was lockt) entring into the Room, through the door, five Appearances of very fine and lovely Women, they were of excellent stature, and their dresses seemed very fine, but covered all but their faces, with thin, white Vails: whose skirts trailed largely on the floor. They entered in a file one after the other, and in that posture walked round the Room, till the foremost came, and stood by that side of the Bed where I lay, (with my left hand over the side of the Bed; for my head rested on that arm, and I determined not to alter the posture I was in) she struck me upon that hand with a blow that felt very soft, but I did never remember whether it were cold or hot; I demanded in the name of the Blessed Trinity what business they had there, but received no answer; then I spoke to Mr C. Sir, do you see what fair Guests we have come to visit us: Upon which they all disappeared: I found him in some kind of Agony, and was forced to grasp him on the breast with my right hand (which was next him underneath the Bed-cloaths) before I could obtain speech of him; then he told me that he had seen the fair Guests I spoke of, and had heard me speak to them; but withal said, that he was not able to speak sooner unto me, being extreamly affrighted at the sight of a dreadful Monster, which assuming a shape betwixt that of a Lyon, and a Bear, attempted to come upon the Beds foot. I told him, I thanked God nothing so frightful had presented itself to me; but I hoped (through his assistance) not to dread the Ambages of Hell. It was a long time before I could compose him to sleep, and though he had had many disturbances in his own Room, and understood of others in the House, yet he acknowledged he had never been so terrify'd, during many years abode there.

– Bovet, *Pandaemonium*, pp. 121–23.

9
The Ghost of Anne Walker

John Ingram, from whose Haunted Homes and Family Traditions of Great Britain *this account is taken, remarks of it, 'Many judicial decisions have been based upon, or influenced by, the presumed testimony of apparitions. These pages contain more than one historical record of such cases, but none more singular than that of Anne Walker, which may be found fully detailed in the works of the famous Dr Henry More, the Platonist.'*

Ghosts who testify against those who have killed them have indeed been recurrent motifs in ghost lore from the seventeenth century to the present day. In the present volume there are three similar stories: see no. 14, 'The Murder of Mary Barwick'; no. 30, 'The Murder of Sergeant Davies'; and no. 59, 'The Red Barn'.

In 1680, according to Dr More, there lived at Lumley, a village near Chester-le-Street, in the county of Durham, a widower named Walker, who was a man in good circumstances. Anne Walker, a young relation of his, kept his house, to the great scandal of the neighbourhood, and, as it proved, with but too good cause. A few weeks before this young woman expected to become a mother, Walker placed her with her aunt, one Dame Cave, in Chester-le-Street, and promised to provide both for her and her future child. One evening towards the end of November, this man, in company with Mark Sharp, an acquaintance of his, came to Dame Cave's door, and told her they had made arrangements for removing her niece to a place where she could remain in safety till her confinement was over. They would not say where it was, but as Walker bore in most respects an excellent character, he was allowed to take the young woman away with him, and he professed to have sent her away with his acquaintance Sharp into Lancashire.

Fourteen days after, runs the story, one Graeme, a fuller who lived about six miles from Lumley, had been engaged till past midnight in his mill; and on coming down-stairs to go home, in the middle of the ground floor he saw a woman, with dishevelled hair, covered with blood, and having five large wounds on her head. Graeme, on recovering a little from his first terror, demanded what the spectre wanted: 'I,' said the apparition, 'am the spirit of Anne Walker,' and then proceeded to tell Graeme the particulars which have already been related as to her removal from her aunt's abode. 'When I was sent away with Mark Sharp,' it proceeded, 'he slew me on such a moor,' naming one that Graeme knew, 'with a collier's pick, threw my body into a coal pit, and hid the pick under the bank; and his shoes and stockings, which were covered with blood, he left in a stream.' The apparition proceeded to tell Graeme that he must give information of this to the nearest Justice of the Peace, and that till this was done he must look to be continually haunted.

Graeme went home very sad; he dared not bring such a charge against a man of so unimpeachable a character as Walker, and yet he as little dared to incur the anger of the spirit that had appeared to him. So, as all weak minds will do, he went on procrastinating, only he took care to leave his mill early, and while in it never to be alone. Notwithstanding this caution on his part, one night, just as it began to be dark, the apparition met him again, in a more terrible shape, and with every circumstance of indignation. Yet he did not even then fulfil its injunction, till, on St Thomas's Eve, as he was walking in his garden, just after sunset, it threatened him so effectually that in the morning he went to a magistrate, and revealed the whole thing.

The place was examined, the body and the pickaxe found, and a warrant was granted against Walker and Sharp. They were, however, admitted to bail, but in August, 1681, their trial came on before Judge Davenport, at Durham. Meanwhile the whole circumstances were known all over the north of England, and the greatest interest was excited by the case. Against Sharp the fact was strong that his shoes and stockings, covered with blood, were found in the place where the murder had been committed; but against Walker, except the accounts received from the ghost, there seemed not a shadow of evidence. Nevertheless, the judge summed up strongly against the prisoners, the jury found them guilty, and the judge pronounced sentence upon them that night, a thing which was unknown in Durham, either before or after. The prisoners were executed, and both died professing their innocence to the last. Judge Davenport was much agitated during the trial, and it was believed, says the historian, 'that the spirit had also appeared to him, as if to supply in his mind the want of legal evidence'.

– Ingram, *Haunted Homes and Family Traditions of Great Britain*, pp. 158–60.

10
The Ghost of Major Sydenham

This is a two-part story that begins in Dulverton (Somerset) and ends at the famous Eton College near Windsor. Joseph Glanvil, who first drew attention to these famous events, says, 'The apparition of the ghost of Major George Sydenham, to Captain William Dyke, [is] taken out of a letter of Mr James Douch of Mongton, to Mr Jos. Glanvil', and that he himself had it from 'the Worthy and Learned Dr Tho. Dyke, a near Kinsman' of the percipient, Captain William Dyke.

Shortly after the Major's death, Dr Thomas Dyke explains, he was asked to go to a house in Dulverton to take care of a sick child. On his way there, he called on his relative, Captain William Dyke, who said he was willing to accompany him because he also had business that night at that house.

I have slightly abridged the story and modernised the punctuation and spelling.

After their arrival at the House [Glanvil writes] they were seasonably conducted to their Lodging; Where, after they had laid a while, the Captain knocked and bids the Servant bring him two of the largest and biggest candles lighted that he could get. Whereupon the Doctor enquires what he meant by this? The Captain answers, 'You know, Cousin, what disputes my Major and I have had touching the Being of a God, and the Immortality of the Soul. In which points we could never be resolved, though we so much sought for and desired it. And therefore it was at length fully agreed between us, that he of us that died first should the third night after his funeral, between the hours of twelve and one come to the little house that is here in the garden, and there give a full account to the survivor touching these matters, who should be sure to be present there at the set time, and to receive a full satisfaction. And this,' says the Captain, 'is the very night, and I am come on purpose to fulfil my promise.'

The Doctor dissuaded him, minding him of the danger of following those strange counsels, for which we could have no warrant, and that the Devil might by some cunning device make such an advantage of this rash attempt, as might work his utter ruin. The Captain replies, that he had solemnly engaged, and that nothing should discourage him: and adds, that if the Doctor would wake a while with him, he would thank him, if not, he might compose himself to his rest; but, for his own part he was resolved to watch, that he might be sure to be present at the hour appointed. To that purpose he sets his watch by him, and as soon as he perceived by it that it was half an hour past eleven, he rises, and taking a candle in each hand, goes out by a back door, of which he had before gotten the key, and walks to the garden-house, where he continued two hours and an half, and at his return declared that he neither saw nor heard anything more than what was usual. But I know, said he, that my Major would surely have come, had he been able.

About six weeks after, the captain rides to Eton to place his son a scholar there, [and] the Doctor went thither with him. They lodged there at an Inn, the sign was the *Christopher*, and tarried two or three nights. The morning before they went thence, the Captain stayed in his chamber longer than he was wont to do before he called upon the Doctor. At length he comes into the Doctor's chamber, but in a visage and form much differing from himself, with his hair and eyes staring, and his whole body shaking and trembling. Whereat the Doctor wondering, presently demanded, 'What is the matter, Cousin captain?' The captain replies, 'I have seen my Major.' At which the Doctor seeming to smile, the Captain immediately confirms it, saying, 'If ever I saw him in my life I saw him but now.' And then he related to the Doctor what had passed, thus: 'This morning after it was light, someone comes to my bedside, and suddenly drawing back the curtains, calls, "*Cap. Cap.*" (which was the term of familiarity that the Major used to call the Captain by) To whom I replied, "What, my Major?" To which he returns, "I could not come at the time appointed, but I am now come to tell you, *That there is a God, and a very just and terrible one, and if you do not turn over a new leaf* (the very expression as is by the Doctor punctually remembered) *you will find it so.*" On the table nearby, there lay a sword which the Major had formerly given me. Now after the Apparition had walked a turn or two about the chamber, he took up the Sword, drew it out, and finding it not to be so clean and bright as it ought, "*Cap. Cap.*" says he, "*this sword did not use to be kept after this fashion when it was mine.*" After which words he suddenly disappeared.'

– Glanvil, *Sadducismus Triumphatus*, pp. 181–84.

11
'Givenni, Givanni'

John Aubrey, whose story I quote below, says, 'This account Sir William Dugdale had from the Bishop of Edinburgh. And this, and the former account he hath writ in a book of miscellanies, which I have seen, and is now reposited with other books of his in the Museum at Oxford.'

Sir William Dugdale did inform me that Major General Middleton (since Lord) went into the Highlands of Scotland, to endeavour to make a party for King Charles I. An old gentleman (that was second-sighted) came and told him, that his endeavour was good, but he would be unsuccessful: and moreover, 'that they would put the King to death: And that several other attempts would be made, but all in vain: but that his son would come in, but not reign; but at last would be restored.' This Lord Middleton had a great friendship with the Laird Bocconi, and they had made an agreement, that the first of them that died should appear to the other in extremity. The Lord Middleton was taken prisoner at Worcester fight, and was prisoner in the Tower of London, under three locks. Lying in his bed pensive, Bocconi appeared to him; my Lord Middleton asked him if he were dead or alive? he said, dead, and that he was a ghost; and told him, that within three days he should escape, and he did so, in his wife's cloaths. When he had done his message, he gave a frisk, and said,

Givenni Givanni 'tis very strange,
In the world to see so sudden a change.

And then gathered up and vanished.

– Aubrey, *Miscellanies*, pp. 80–81.

12
The Headless Bear

Richard Baxter presents this double bill of stories from the West Midlands, in which terrifying spectres frighten unbelievers into honest and religious lives. 'Kederminster' is modern-day Kidderminster (Worcestershire).

Simon Jones, a strong and healthful man of Kederminster (no way inclined to melancholy or any fancies), hath oft told me, that being a souldier for the King in the war against the parliament, in a clear moon-shine night, as he stood sentinel in the Colledge Green at Worcester, something like a headless bear appeared to him, and so effrighted him, that he laid down his arms soon after, and returned home to his trade, and while I was there afterward, which was fourteen years, lived honestly, religiously, and without blame, and is I think yet living, which mindeth me of that which followeth, though to me not known.

When I was young, most credible and religious persons born in Wilden-Hall near Wolverhampton in Staffordshire, oft told me ... that one Richard White, a smith of Wilden-Hall, was a prophane, atheistical man, and believing that there was no devils, in his cups would wish he could once see the devil, if there were such a thing; and that suddenly he changed his life, and became a professor of zeal, and strictness in religion, and told them, that in a clear moon-shine night the devil in the shape of a great ugly man stood by his bedside, opening the curtains, and looking him in the face, and at last took up the blanket, and sometime smiled on him, and then was more ugly; and after a while (in which he lay in great terror) the apparition vanished, and he was affrighted into the aforesaid change of life ...

– Baxter, *The Certainty of the World of Spirits*, pp. 64–66.

13
'Here She Comes!'

According to John Aubrey, this story was investigated by no less a personage than King Charles I. Aubrey had it from his 'worthy friend Mr Monson', who in turn had it from the brother and father of the percipient.

Sir John Burroughes being sent envoy to the Emperor by King Charles I did take his eldest son Caisho Burroughes along with him, and taking his journey through Italy, left his son at Florence, to learn the language; where he having an intrigue with a beautiful courtisan (mistress of the Grand Duke), their familiarity became so public, that it came to the Duke's ear, who took a resolution to have him murdered; but Caisho having had timely notice of the Duke's design, by some of the English there, immediately left the city without acquainting his mistress with it, and came to England; whereupon the Duke being disappointed of his revenge, fell upon his mistress in most reproachful language; she on the other side, resenting the sudden departure of her gallant, of whom she was most passionately enamoured, killed herself. At the same moment that she expired, she did appear to Caisho, at his lodgings in London ... giving him an account of her resentments of his ingratitude to her, in leaving her so suddenly, and exposing her to the fury of the Duke, not omitting her own tragical exit, adding withal, that he should be slain in a duel, which accordingly happened; and thus she appeared to him frequently ... As often as she did appear, he would cry out with great shrieking, and trembling of his body, as anguish of mind, saying, 'O God! Here she comes, she comes,' and at this rate she appeared till he was killed; she appeared to him the morning before he was killed. Some of my acquaintance have told me, that he was one of the most beautiful men in England, and very valiant, but proud and blood-thirsty.

This story was so common, that King Charles I sent for Caisho Burroughes' father, whom he examined as to the truth of the matter; who did ... aver the matter of fact to be true, so that the King thought it worth his while to send to Florence, to enquire at what time this unhappy lady killed herself; it was found to be the same minute that she first appeared to Caisho.

– Aubrey, *Miscellanies*, pp. 74–75.

14
The Murder of Mary Barwick

In introducing this story John Aubrey remarks that 'as murder is one of the greatest crimes that man can be guilty of, so it is no less strangely and providentially discovered, when privately committed. The foul criminal believes himself secure, because there was no witness of the fact ... [but] ... the very ghosts ... cannot rest quiet in their graves, till they have made the detection themselves'.

The first 'remarkable example of this', he says, 'was committed by William Barwick, upon the body of Mary Barwick, his wife, at the same time big with child'. Mary was supposed to have been killed in the grounds of Cawood Castle, near Selby, North Yorkshire. The castle itself would have already been demolished at the time of the murder (it was pulled down in 1646). All that remains now is its fifteenth-century gatehouse, the moats, and two of its five original fishponds. It seems likely that Mary Barwick was drowned in one of these fishponds.

For other stories of so-called 'spectral evidence' against murderers see no. 9 'The Ghost of Anne Walker' in this section. The eighteenth-century story of the Murder of Sergeant Davies (no. 30) and the nineteenth-century story of Maria Marten ('The Red Barn', no. 59) are further examples. Note, too, that the ghost of Jan Tregeagle (no. 66) was brought back as a witness in a case involving a land dispute.

The murder was committed on Palm-Monday, being the fourteenth of April, about two of the clock in the afternoon, at which time the said Barwick having [dragged] his wife along 'till he came to a certain close, within sight of Cawood-Castle, where he found the conveniency of a pond, he threw her by force into the water, and when she was drowned, and drawn forth again by himself upon the bank of the pond, had the cruelty to behold the motion of the infant, yet warm in her womb. This done, he concealed the body, as it may readily be supposed, among the bushes, that usually encompass a pond, and the next night, when it grew duskish, fetching a hay-spade from a rick that stood in a close, he made a hole by the side of the pond, and there slightly buried the woman in her cloaths.

Having thus despatched two at once, and thinking himself secure (because unseen), he went the same day to his brother-in-law, one Thomas Lofthouse of Rufforth, within three miles of York ... and told him he had [taken] his wife to one Richard Harrison's house in Selby, who was his uncle, and would take care of her. But Heaven would not be so deluded, but raised up the ghost of the murdered woman to make the discovery. And therefore it was upon the Easter

Tuesday following, about two of the clock in the after-noon, the forementioned Lofthouse having occasion to water a quickset hedge, not far from his house; as he was going for the second pail full, an apparition went before him in the shape of a woman, and soon after sat down upon a rising green grass-plat, right over against the pond: he walked by her as he went to the pond; and as he returned with the pail from the pond, looking sideways to see whether she continued in the same place, he found she did; and that she seemed to dandle something in her lap, that looked like a white bag (as he thought) which he did not observe before. So soon as he had emptied his pail, he went into his yard, and stood still to try whether he could see her again, but she was vanished.

In this information he says, that the woman seemed to be habited in a brown coloured petticoat, waistcoat, and a white hood; such a one as his wife's sister usually wore, and that her countenance looked extreamly pale and wan, with her teeth in sight, but no gums appearing, and that her physiognomy was like to that of his wife's sister, who was wife to William Barwick.

But notwithstanding the ghastliness of the apparition, it seems it made so little impression in Lofthouse's mind, that he thought no more of it, neither did he speak to any body concerning it, 'till the same night as he was at his family duty of prayer, that the apparition returned again to his thoughts, and discomposed his devotion; so that after he had made an end of his prayers, he told the whole story of what he had seen to his wife, who laying circumstances together, immediately inferred that her sister was either drowned, or otherwise murdered, and desired her husband to look [for] her the next day, which was Wednesday in Easter week. Upon this, Lofthouse recollecting what Barwick had told him of his [taking] his wife to his uncle at Selby, repaired to Harrison before mentioned, but found all that Barwick had said to be false; for that Harrison had neither heard of Barwick, nor his wife, neither did he know anything of them. Which notable circumstance, together with that other of the apparition, encreased his suspicions to that degree, that now concluding his wife's sister was murdered, he went to the Lord Mayor of York; and having obtained his warrant, got Barwick apprehended, who was no sooner brought before the Lord Mayor, but his own conscience then accusing him, he acknowledged the whole matter, as it has been already related, as it appears by his examination and confession herewith printed: to which are also annexed the informations of Lofthouse, in like manner taken before the Lord Mayor of York, for a further testimony and confirmation of what is here set down.

On Wednesday the sixteenth of September, 1690, the criminal, William Barwick, was brought to his trial, before the Honourable Sir John Powel, Knight, one of the judges of the northern circuit, at the assizes holden at York, where the prisoner pleaded not guilty to his indictment: but upon the evidence of Thomas Lofthouse, and his wife, and a third person, that the woman was found buried in her cloaths in the Close by the pond side, agreeable to the prisoner's confession, and that she had several bruises on her head, occasioned by the blows the murderer had given her, to keep her under water: and upon reading the prisoner's confession before the Lord Mayor of York, attested by the clerk, who wrote the confession, and who swore the prisoner's owning and signing it for truth, he was found guilty, and sentenced to death, and afterwards ordered to be hanged in chains.

All the defence which the prisoner made, was only this, that he was threatened into the confession that he had made, and was in such a consternation, that he did not know what he said or did. But then it was sworn by two witnesses, that there was no such thing as any threatening made use of; but that he made a free and voluntary confession, only with this addition at first; that he told the Lord Mayor, he had sold his wife for five shillings; but not being able to name either the person or the place where she might be produced, that was looked upon as too frivolous to outweigh circumstances, that were proofs too apparent.

– Aubrey, *Miscellanies*, pp. 96–99.

15
The Phantom Battle of Edgehill

In his Remaines of Gentilisme and Judaisme *(1686–87), John Aubrey observed that 'Warres doe not only extinguish Religion and Laws, but Superstitions; and no suffimen is a greater fumigator of Phantosmes than gunpowder'. The evidence of this and other legends, however, would seem to challenge this statement. Among many accounts of phantom battles the spectral replay of the battle of Edgehill, the first pitched battle of the English Civil War (1642–51), must be one of the most popular. Three of the stories in this section also date from this unsettled period – no. 11, 'Givenni, Givanni'; no. 12, 'The Headless Bear'; and no. 19, 'The Wraith of Mr Mohun'.*

The battle of Edgehill was fought on 23 October 1642 in south Warwickshire near Kineton. Casualties were high – 500 dead and 1,500 wounded – but neither side were able to gain ascendancy. After the battle the King resumed his march on London from his temporary capital at York.

The legend has been much anthologised; other sources include: Katharine Briggs, The Folklore of the Cotswolds; *T. F. Thiselton-Dyer,* The Ghost World; *Alasdair Alpin MacGregor,* Phantom Footsteps; *John Ingram* Haunted Homes and Family Traditions of Great Britain; *and Christina Hole,* Haunted England.

The account reproduced here, which comes from George Grenville, Baron Nugent, is almost contemporaneous with the supposed events. The text has been a little abridged, but the original spelling and punctuation have been retained.

Edge-Hill, in the very confines of Warwickshire, neere unto [Kineton] [was] where, in defence of the Kingdomes lawes and libertie, was fought a bloody conflict between his Majesties and the Parliaments forces; at this Edge-Hill, in the very place where the battell was strucken, have since, and doth appeare, strange and portentuous Apparitions of two jarring and contrary Armies [...] Between twelve and one of the clock in the morning was heard by some sheepherds, and other countrey-men, and travellers, first the sound of drummes afar off, and the noyse of souldiers, as it were, giving out their last groanes; at which they were much amazed, and amazed stood still, till it seemed, by the neerenesse of the noyse, to approach them; at which too much affrighted, they sought to withdraw as fast as possibly they could; but then, on the sudden, whilest they were in their cogitations, appeared in the ayre the same incorporeall souldiers that made those clamours, and immediately, with Ensignes display'd, Drummes beating, Musquets going off, Cannons discharged, Horses neyghing, which also to these men were visible, the alarum or entrance to this game of death was strucke up, one Army, which gave the first charge, having the Kings colours, and the other the Parliaments ... and so pell mell to it they went; the battell that appeared to the Kings forces seeming at first to have the best, but afterwards to be put into apparent rout; but till two or three in the morning in equall scale continued this dreadful fight, the clattering of Armes, noyse of Cannons, cries of souldiers, so amazing and terrifying the poore men, that they could not believe they were mortall, or give credit to their eares and eyes; runne away they durst not, for feare of being made a prey to these infernall souldiers, and so they, with much feare and affright, stayed to behold the successe of the businesse, which at last suited to this effect: after some three houres fight, that Army which carryed the Kings colours withdrew, or rather appeared to flie; the other remaining, as it were, masters of the field, stayed a good space triumphing, and expressing all the signes of joy and conquest, and then, with all their Drummes, Trumpets, Ordnance, and Souldiers, vanished [...]

The next night they appeared not, nor all that week, so that the dwellers thereabout were in good hope they had for ever departed; but on the ensuing Saturday night, in the same place, and at the same houre, they were again seene with far greater tumult, fighting in the manner afore-mentioned for foure houres, or verie neere, and then vanished, appearing againe on Sunday night, and performing the same actions of hostilitie and bloodshed [...] and so successively the next Saturday and Sunday the same tumults and prodigious sights and actions were put in the state and condition they were formerly. The rumour whereof comming to his Majestie at Oxford, he immediately dispatched thither Colonell Lewis Kirke, Captaine Dudley, Captaine Wainman, and three other Gentlemen of credit, to take the full view and notice of the said businesse, who, first hearing the true attestation and relation of Mr Marshall and others, staid there till Saturday night following, wherein they heard and saw the fore-mentioned prodigies, and so on Sunday, distinctly knowing divers of the apparitions or incorporeall substances by their faces, as that of Sir Edmund Verney, and others that were there slaine; of which upon oath they made testimony to his Majestie. What this does portend God only knoweth, and time perhaps will discover; but doubtlessly it is a signe of his wrath against this Land, for these civill wars, which He in his good time finish, and send a sudden peace between his Majestie and Parliament. – Finis.

– Grenville, *Some Memorials of John Hamden*, Appendix E.

16
Stripped

This racy story is the twelfth 'Relation' in Richard Bovet's Pandaemonium *(1684). It is, Bovet says, 'perhaps one of the most stupendious accounts of this nature that have been heard of; I could say much more, only for the regard and Honour I ought to bear to the Family, I dare not name them, unless I had their leave, but the thing is so well known to all that were in the house at the time, which were more than thirty, and by them imparted to so many others, that it is beyond the skill of the greatest Cavaller to contest it.' The original spelling and punctuation have been retained.*

I had occasion to make mention of a Noblemans House in the West of England, and to give two Relations of what passed there of my own knowledge: I shall now add another, known to the Lady, and all the Family; which is thus.

One night, as we were at Supper, one of the Ladies Footmen complained he was pained in his Head, whereupon he had orders to go to Bed, which he did some hours before the rest of the Family. His Lodging was by the side of a fair Gallery, where there were several Alcoves, with Beds, for the Servants, and they were planted near Sir F.'s Lodging. When the Lady was disposed to go to her Chamber, the other Company waited on her up the Stairs (most of us lodging the same way) we passed into the foresaid Gallery, and when we came over against the Alcove, where the Page was, we found the door of it open, and out of it issued a steam, which by the light of the Candles appeared like a thick Fog: which occasioned some of us to look into the Room, where we saw the poor young Man lying speechless on the Bed, his Eyes were staring very wide, and fixed on one side of the Room, his Hands were clutched, his Hair erected, and his whole body in so violent a sweat, as if he had been in the *Bagnio*; all the Clothes of the Bed were flung, some in one part of the Room, and some in another, his very shirt was drawn off his Body, and cast into one side of the Room; and it was near half an hour before he could recollect himself, and gather breath, so as to speak to us: At length, having taken somewhat to recall his Spirits, he gave us this surprising account of what had past from the time he went to Bed, which we guess'd to be about three hours. He told us that he lay about half an hour, endeavouring to compose himself to sleep, but could not, because of the pain in his Head, that about that time there came into the Room to him two [missing word] in the appearance of very beautiful young Women, whose presence enlightned the place, as if it had been day, though there was no Candle near it. That they endeavoured to come into the Bed to him, being one on the one side, the other on the other side thereof, which he resisted with all the power he could, striking at them several times with his Fists, but could feel nothing but empty shadows; yet were they so strong, that they drew all the Bed-clothes off him, though he endeavoured with all his force to hold them, that after that they had stripped him of his shirt; and he had contested so long with them, that he concluded within himself he should die under their violencies, during all that time he had no power to speak, or call for aid; but was at last reduced to that condition wherein we found him. Some were ordered to continue that night; and the next day he was bleeded, having been much bruised in the Conflict; however he had no sickness after it, nor do I hear that ever after he had any disturbance from them.

– Bovet, *Pandaemonium*, pp. 132–33.

17
The Wraith of John Donne's Wife

John Donne (1573–1631), priest and poet, was created Dean of St Paul's in 1621 and is often remembered for his 'no man is an island' sermon. He is generally considered the most eminent of the seventeenth-century 'metaphysical' poets, a group which also includes George Herbert and Andrew Marvell.

In 1601 Donne secretly married Anne More, the daughter of Sir George More, Lieutenant of the Tower (of London) – an offence for which Sir George had him imprisoned alongside the priest who had married them and the witness to the ceremony. Anne died in 1617 after bearing Donne twelve children, seven of whom survived. He did not remarry.

In his Life of Donne *(1639), Izaak Walton says that the events recorded below happened while Donne was accompanying Lord Haye on a mission to the French King Henry IV, but a footnote to the 1898 edition of this work points out that the dates do not tally – Lord Haye did not go to Paris until 1616; by then both Henry IV and Sir Robert Drury were dead (Henry died in 1610, and Sir Robert in 1615).*

At this time of Mr Donne's and his wife's living in Sir Robert Drury's house in Drury-Lane, the Lord Haye was by King James sent upon a glorious embassy, to the then French King Henry IV, and Sir Robert put on a sudden resolution to accompany him to the French Court, and to be present at his audience there. And Sir Robert put on as sudden a resolution, to subject Mr Donne to be his companion in that journey; and this desire was suddenly made known to his wife, who was then with child, and otherwise under so dangerous a habit of body, as to her health, that she protested an unwillingness to allow him any absence from her; saying her divining soul boded her some ill in his absence, and therefore desired him not to leave her. This made Mr Donne lay aside all thoughts of his journey, and really to resolve against it. But Sir Robert became restless in his persuasions for it, and Mr Donne was so generous as to think he had sold his liberty, when he had received so many charitable kindnesses from him, and told his wife so; who, therefore, with an unwilling willingness, did give a faint consent to the journey, which was proposed to be but for two months: within a few days after this resolve, the Ambassador, Sir Robert, and Mr Donne, left London, and were the twelfth day got safe to Paris. Two days after their arrival there, Mr Donne was left alone in the room, where Sir Robert and he, with some others, had dined: to this place Sir Robert returned within half an hour, and as he left, so he found Mr Donne alone, but in such an extacy, and so altered as to his looks, as amazed Sir Robert to behold him, insomuch as he earnestly desired Mr Donne to declare what had befallen him in the short time of his absence? to which Mr Donne was not able to make a present answer, but after a long and perplexed pause, said, 'I have seen a dreadful vision since I saw you: I have seen my dear wife pass twice by me through this room, with her hair hanging about her shoulders, and a dead child in her arms; this I have seen since I saw you.' To which Sir Robert replied, 'Sure Sir, you have slept since I saw you, and this is the result of some melancholy dream, which I desire you to forget, for you are now awake.' To which Mr Donne's reply was, 'I cannot be surer that I now live, than that I have not slept since I saw you, and am sure that at her second appearing, she stopt and lookt me in the face and vanished.'

Rest and sleep had not altered Mr Donne's opinion the next day, for he then affirmed this vision with a more deliberate, and so confirmed a confidence, that he inclined Sir Robert to a faint belief, that the vision was true. It is truly said, that desire and doubt have no rest, and it proved so with Sir Robert, for he immediately sent a servant to Drury-House, with a charge to hasten back and bring him word whether Mrs Donne were alive? and if alive, in what condition she was as to her health. The twelfth day the messenger returned with this account – that he found and left Mrs Donne very sad, sick in her bed, and that, after a long and dangerous labour, she had been delivered of a dead child: and upon examination, the apparition proved to be the same day, and about the very hour, that Mr Donne affirmed he saw her pass by him in his chamber.

– Walton, *The Life of Dr Donne*, pp. 33–35.

18
The Wraith of Mary Goffe

Chapter 7 of Richard Baxter's The Certainty of the World of Spirits *is composed of what Baxter calls 'Letters and Relations concerning Apparitions and Witchcrafts'. It begins with a letter from 'Mr Thomas Tilson, Minister of Aylesworth in Kent', dated 1691. 'Being informed that you are writing about Witchcraft and Apparitions,' the Reverend Tilson says, 'I take the freedom, though a Stranger, to send you this following Relation.'*

It is one of two versions of the events which Baxter prints.

Mary, the wife of John Goffe, of Rochester, being afflicted with a long illness, removed to her father's house at West Mulling, which is about nine miles distant from her own: there she died, June the 4th, this present year, 1691.

The day before her departure, she grew very impatiently desirous to see her two children, whom she had left at home, in the care of a nurse. She prayed her husband to hire a horse, for she must go home, and die with the children. When they persuaded her to the contrary, telling her she was not to be taken out of her bed, nor able to sit on horseback; she entreated them, however, to try, 'If I cannot sit,' said she, 'I will lie all along upon the horse, for I must go and see my poor babes.'

A minister, who lives in the town, was with her at ten o'clock that night, to whom she expressed good hopes in the mercy of God, and a willingness to die: 'But,' said she, 'It is my misery that I cannot see my children.'

Between one and two-a-clock in the morning she fell into a trance. Widow Turner, who watched with her that night, says, that her eyes were open and fixed, and her jaw fallen; she put her hand upon her mouth and nostrils, but could perceive no breath, she thought her to be in a fit, and doubted whether she were alive or dead.

The next day the dying woman told her mother that she had been at home with her children. 'That is impossible,' said the mother, 'for you have been here in bed all the while.' 'Yes,' replied the other, 'but I was with them all night, when I was asleep.'

The nurse at Rochester, Widow Alexander by name, affirms, and says she will take her oath on't before a magistrate, and receive the sacrament upon it, that a little before two-a-clock that morning, she saw the likeness of the said Mary Goffe come out of the next chamber (where the elder child lay in a bed by itself, the door being left open), and stood by her bedside for about a quarter of an hour: the younger child was there lying by her: her eyes moved, and her mouth went, but she said nothing. The nurse moreover says, that she was perfectly awake, it was then daylight, being one of the longest days in the year. She sate up in her bed, and looked steadfastly upon the apparition; in that time she heard the bridge-clock strike two, and a while after said, 'In the name of the Father, Son, and Holy Ghost, what art thou?' Thereupon the appearance removed, and went away: she slipped on her cloaths and followed, but what became on't she cannot tell.

Then, and not before, she began to be grievously affrighted, and went out of doors, and walked upon the wharf (the house is just by the river side) for some hours, only going in now and then to look at the children. At five-a-clock she went to a neighbour's house, and knocked at the door, but they would not rise; at six she went again, then they rose and let her in. She related to them all that had pass'd, they would have persuaded her she was mistaken, or dreamt, but she confidently affirmed, 'If ever I saw her in all my life I saw her this night.'

– Baxter, *The Certainty of the World of Spirits*, pp. 96–100.

19
The Wraith of Mr Mohun

John Aubrey's chapter on 'Apparitions', pages 70–105 of his Miscellanies, *is a great rag-bag of stories and legends about the appearances of fetches, wraiths, angels and spectres to a range of personages that include St Augustine, King Charles the Simple of France, King Edward the Confessor of England, and a 'Mr Fynes Moryson' who said that when he was at Prague the apparition of his father came to him at 'the very moment' of his death.*

In the present volume there are a number of stories of apparitions who appear at the moment of death or in times of crisis – in this section, see no. 18, 'The Wraith of Mary Goffe'; and no. 17, 'The Wraith of John Donne's Wife'. See also no. 22, 'The Birkbeck Ghost'; and no. 35 'The Wynyard Wraith'. For a similar modern story see no. 93, '"Father's Dead!"'

Anno 1647, the Lord Mohun's son and heir (a gallant gentleman, valiant, and a great master of fencing and horsemanship), had a quarrel with Prince Griffin; there was a challenge, and they were to fight on horse-back in Chelsea-fields in the morning: Mr Mohun went accordingly to meet him; but about Ebury-Farm, he was met by some who quarrelled with him and pistoled him; it was believed, by the order of Prince Griffin; for he was sure, that Mr Mohun, being so much the better horse-man, &c. would have killed him, had they fought.

In James-street, in Covent-Garden, did then lodge a gentlewoman, a handsome woman, but common, who was Mr Mohun's sweet heart. Mr Mohun was murdered about ten o'clock in the morning; and at that very time, his mistress being in bed, saw Mr Mohun come to her bed-side, draw the curtain, look upon her and go away; she called after him, but no answer: she knocked for her maid, asked her for Mr Mohun; she said she did not see him, and had the key of her chamber-door in her pocket. This account my friend aforesaid had from the gentle-woman's own mouth, and her maid's.

– Aubrey, *Miscellanies*, pp. 76–77.

20
'You Say True. You Are in the Right'

Joseph Glanvil says that this narrative, Relation 15 of his Sadducismus Triumphatus *(1682), 'was sent in a letter to J. C. for Dr H. More, from Mr Thomas Alcock of Shear-Hampton ... I am, saith he, very confident of the truth of the Story: for I had it from a very good Lady, the eldest Daughter of the said John Mallet ... and only Aunt to the Countess of Rochester, who knew all the parties; and have heard Dr Raymond and Mr Carlisle relate it often with amazement, being both persons of Credit.'*

Mr John Bourne, for his skill, care and honesty, was made by his neighbour John Mallet esq. of Enmore, the chief of his trustees for his son ... and the rest of his children in [their] minority. He had the reputation of a worthy good man, and was commonly taken notice of for an habitual saying, by way of interjection almost to anything, 'You say true, You say true. You are in the right.' This Mr Bourne fell sick at his house in Durley in the year 1654 and Dr Raymond of Oake was sent for, who after some time gave the said Mr Bourne over. And he had not now spoke in twenty four hours, when the said Dr Raymond, and Mrs Carlisle (Mr Bourne's nephew's wife) ... sitting by his bedside, the doctor opened the curtains at the bed's feet, to give him air; when on a sudden, to the horror and amazement of Dr Raymond and Mrs Carlisle, the great iron chest by the window at his bed's feet with three locks to it (in which were all the writings and evidences of the said Mr Mallet's estate) began to open, first one lock, then another, then the third. Afterwards the lid of the said iron chest lifted up itself, and stood wide open. Then the patient Mr Bourne, who had not spoke in twenty four hours, lifted himself up also, and looking upon the chest, cried, 'You say true. You say true. You are in the right. I'll be with you by and by.' So the patient lay down, and spoke no more. Then the chest fell again of itself, and locked itself one lock after the other, as the three locks [had] opened; and they tried to knock it open and could not, and Mr Bourne died within an hour after.

– Glanvil, *Sadducismus Triumphatus*, pp. 451–52.

Top right: 1. *Portrait of Revd Richard Baxter (1615–91), author of* The Certainty of the World of Spirits *(1691)*
See 'Colonel Bowen Visits His Wife', story no. 4; 'The Wraith of Mary Goffe', story no. 18; and 'The Headless Bear', story no. 12. Source: *Practical Works of the Rev Richard Baxter* by William Orme, internet archive.

Bottom right: 2. *The Crimean war memorial outside Westminster Cathedral*
The old Gatehouse once stood in this spot, and it was there that Captain Henry Bell was imprisoned for ten years, five of which were spent translating the works of Martin Luther. See 'Captain Henry Bell Explains', story no. 3.

Above: 3. *Memorial plaque to John Ruddle in the south aisle of St Mary Magdalene, Launceston, Cornwall*
See 'Dorothy Dingley', story no. 7.

Left: 4. *South porch of the church of St Mary Magdalene, Launceston, Cornwall*
The ghost-layer John Ruddle was vicar here from 1663 to his death in 1698. See 'Dorothy Dingley', story no. 7.

5. *A quiet corner of College Green, Worcester*
It was here, in the grounds of the Cathedral school, that a 'strong and healthful' man of Kidderminster saw an apparition 'something like a headless bear' and resolved to amend his life. See 'The Headless Bear', story no. 12.

6. *Gatehouse to Cawood Castle, near Selby, North Yorkshire*
See 'The Murder of Mary Barwick', story no. 14.

Above: 7. *Old St Paul's Cathedral, London, destroyed by the Great Fire of London in 1666*
The priest and poet John Donne (1572–1631) was appointed Dean here in 1621. See 'The Wraith of John Donne's Wife', story no. 17. Source: Robert Chambers, *The Book of Days*, vol. 1, p. 423.

Opposite above: 8. *Modern-day Cock Lane, Smithfield, London*
In the mid-eighteenth century Cock Lane was the location of a poltergeist haunting which became a *cause célèbre* and attracted the interest of poet and novelist Oliver Goldsmith. See 'The Cock Lane Poltergeist', story no. 23.

9. *Llyn Gwyn near Rhayader, Powys*

It was into this pool that the Great Giant of Henllys was thrown after seven pious parsons had transformed him into a fly and shut him in a tobacco box. See 'The Great Giant of Henllys', story no. 26.

Left: 10. *Epworth Old Rectory, Isle of Axholme, Lincolnshire* This Queen Anne Grade I listed building was the home of the Wesley family in the early eighteenth century. This gracious house seems an unlikely place for a haunting, especially as it was only a few years old in 1716 when the disturbances took place (it had been rebuilt in 1709 after a fire had destroyed the previous building). See 'The Haunting of Epworth Parsonage', story no. 28.

Below: 11. *The Tithe Barn at Leigh Court, Worcestershire* The ghost of 'Old Coles' is said to drive through this massive building. The photograph shows two of its four huge doors standing open, and fourteen of its eighteen cruck blades. See 'Old Coles', story no. 32.

PART 2

The Eighteenth Century

Introduction

By the middle years of the eighteenth century, the battle for belief in ghosts and spirits would appear to be over, but despite such ideas being laughed at publicly, in private many people continued to believe in ghosts and swap stories about them. The works of seventeenth-century authors such as Joseph Glanvil (1636–80), Richard Bovet (b. *c.* 1641) and George Sinclair (d. 1696) were still to be seen in tradesmen's shops and farmers' houses, and exerted a considerable influence on the minds of young people.

Likewise, an account of the apparition of Mrs Veal, by Daniel Defoe (1659–1713), first published in 1706, ran to over twenty-five editions and did not finally go out of print until 1965. Defoe's *Political History of the Devil* ran to eighteen editions between 1726 and 1843, and the book he wrote under the pen-name Andrew Morton, *Secrets of the Invisible World Disclos'd,* was reissued four times in eleven years. So there are many lively stories of haunting to be had in the so-called Age of Enlightenment, and the stories show how strong popular interest was in such things. More than one of the accounts in this section describes crowds of people going ghost-hunting or assembling outside (or sometimes even inside) houses where a poltergeist was thought to be operating.

One of the ironic consequences of the public scepticism of the age was that stories of supernatural happenings often became rather lengthy. The *cause célèbre* of the mid-century, the case of the Cock Lane Ghost, merited a pamphlet all of its own attributed to no less a person than the poet and playwright Oliver Goldsmith (1730–74); and John Wesley (1703–91), the founder of Methodism, used a lengthy article in the *Arminian Magazine* to recount the history of the haunting of his family home. Extracts from both these accounts are included in the sample of eighteenth-century stories in this section, as is the story of the 'Wynyard Wraith', which was equally well known and much discussed in the closing years of the century. The reason for the length of these narratives, one would guess, is that the storytellers expected to be met with scorn or scepticism so they were careful to include as much authentication and circumstantial details as they could to back up their stories.

Both the Cock Lane Ghost and the Haunting of Epworth Parsonage were stories of poltergeist activity, a theme which had been carried over from the preceding century and would continue to dominate ghost-lore for two centuries more. In other typical stories of the age, we can come across other enduring motifs – the wraiths of the newly-dead or dying, supernatural warnings, and ghosts who reveal murder. Other motifs, if not exactly new, were given more prominence in eighteenth-century stories than previously and would become more and more prevalent in the nineteenth century. Among these were stories about headless horsemen and ghosts in animal form.

The latter were thought to be particularly dangerous because they were the spirits of evil-doers. The way to deal with them, if the stories are to be believed, was to subdue the unruly spirit, cork him in a bottle and throw him into deep water, a local 'bottomless pool' or the Red Sea. Several stories in this section show how this was to be achieved: twelve venerable and holy men, armed with candles and Prayer Books, must assemble at midnight in the church, draw a protective circle around themselves, and wait for the ghost to appear. They must then 'pray him down' reducing him to successively smaller forms (from a bull to a fly, for example) until he can be captured, imprisoned and disposed of. The candles, symbols of faith, must not be allowed to go out until the evil spirit has been subdued. The fullest such accounts can be found in this section in the story of 'The Great Giant of Henllys' (no. 26) and its nineteenth-century sister-story 'The Roaring Bull of Bagbury' (no. 60). Stories that show such ceremonies in truncated form also appear later, notably in 'For Ever and Aye' (no. 42) and 'The Laying of Benjie Gear' (no. 47).

21
An Apparition Saves a Drunkard's Life

This account by William Moore of Redruth, Cornwall, from a letter dated 22 January 1784, was published in the Arminian Magazine *(founded by John Wesley in 1778).*

St Just is the most westerly town in mainland Britain.

A few days ago, I visited John Thomas, of St Just in Cornwall. He is about sixty-two years of age, and has been a notorious drunkard the greatest part of his life. He told me that on Sunday 21 December 1783, about 7 o'clock in the evening, he left San Crete in order to go to St Just. As it was dark he missed his way, and about midnight fell into a pit about five fathoms deep. On his being missing his friends made diligent search for him, but to no purpose. The next Sabbath day, as one of his neighbours was going to seek his sheep, he saw, at some distance, the appearance of a man sitting on the bank which had been thrown up in digging the pit. On drawing near he saw the apparition go round to the other side of the bank. When he came to the place he could see no one; but heard a human voice in the bottom of the pit. Thinking that some smugglers had got down to hide their liquors, he went on; but coming back the same way he again heard the voice. He now listened more attentively, and as he could hear but one voice, he concluded it was John Thomas who was missing, and on calling to him, he found he was not mistaken. On this he went and got help, and soon got him out of the pit. But as he had been there near eight days he was very low when he was got out; but is now in a fair way to do well. In the bottom of the pit he found a small current of water; which he drank freely of. This, in all likelihood, was the means of keeping him alive. It is said that several other persons saw the apparition, but took no notice of it. As I am not fond of crediting stories of this kind on common report, I resolved to get the account from his own mouth.

– Quoted in Hole, *Haunted England*, p. 132.

22
The Birkbeck Ghost

'One of the most striking and best authenticated cases on record is known as the Birkbeck Ghost,' T. F. Thiselton-Dyer writes of this account of a dying mother's visit to her far-away children (but note its similarity to story no. 18, Richard Baxter's seventeenth-century account of the wraith of Mary Goffe). Thiselton-Dyer says the account was provided by W. T. Stead and printed in the Proceedings of the Society for Psychical Research *under the title 'Real Ghost Stories'. Though he cites a page number, he doesn't give the issue or the date, and I have not been able to trace the original. Consequently, it is Thiselton-Dyer's account that I give here.*

Settle is a market town in the Yorkshire Dales; Cockermouth is a considerable distance away on the western edge of the Lake District in Cumbria.

In 1789, Mrs Birkbeck, wife of William Birkbeck, banker, of Settle, and a member of the Society of Friends, was taken ill and died at Cockermouth while returning from a journey to Scotland, which she had undertaken alone – her husband and three children, aged seven, five, and four years respectively, remaining at Settle. The friends at whose house the death occurred made notes of every circumstance attending Mrs Birkbeck's last hours, so that the accuracy of the several statements as to time as well as place was beyond the doubtfulness of man's memory, or of any even unconscious attempt to bring them into agreement with each other. One morning, between seven and eight o'clock, the relation to whom the care of the children had been entrusted, and who kept a minute journal of all that concerned them, went into their bedroom, as usual, and found them all sitting up in bed in great excitement and delight. 'Mamma has been here,' they cried; and the little one said, 'She called, "Come, Esther!"' Nothing could make them doubt the fact, and it was carefully noted down to entertain the mother when she came home. That same morning, as their mother lay on her dying bed at Cockermouth, she said, 'I should be ready to go if I could but see my children.' She then closed her eyes, to reopen them, as they thought, no more. But after ten minutes of perfect stillness she looked up brightly, and said, 'I am ready now; I have been with my children'; and at once passed peacefully away. When the notes taken at the two places were compared, the day, hour, and minutes were the same.

– Thiselton-Dyer, *The Ghost World*, pp. 875–76.

23
The Cock Lane Poltergeist

It was in the context of public scepticism but private belief that the Cock Lane poltergeist excited attention for a full five years during the mid-1700s. The knockings and scratchings at the house in Cock Lane in London were said to be caused by the restless spirit of the common-law wife of Mr K—, who was thought by many (including the lady's family) to have poisoned her in order to come by her small inheritance. The knockings emanated from a young girl, and fashionable London turned out to sit in her bedroom and listen to the manifestations. The case was discussed in a monograph attributed to the poet, novelist and dramatist Oliver Goldsmith. The author's presentation of what he sees as the facts, his sneering language and dismissive logic, are just as interesting as the story itself and entirely representative of the attitudes of his age. Extracts from this pamphlet form the following account.

[O]f all [unjust] accusations few seem so extraordinary, as that which has lately engrossed the attention of the public, and which is still carrying on at an house in Cock Lane near Smithfield. The continuance of the noises, the numbers who have heard them, the perseverance of the girl, and the atrociousness of the murder she [claims] to detect, are circumstances that were never perhaps so favourably united for the carrying on of an imposture before. The credulous are prejudiced by the child's apparent benevolence: her age and ignorance wipe off the imputation of her being able to deceive, and one or two more, who [claim] actually to have seen the apparition, are ready to strengthen her evidence. Upon these grounds, a man, otherwise of a fair character, as will shortly appear, is rendered odious to society, shunned by such as immediately take imputation for guilt, and made unhappy in his family, without having even in law a power of redress [...]

The story of the ghost is in brief, as follows: for some time a knocking and scratching has been heard in the night at Mr P—s's, where Mr K— formerly lodged, to the great terror of the family; and several methods were tried, to discover the imposture, but without success. This knocking and scratching was generally heard in a little room, in which Mr P—s's two children lay; the eldest of which was a girl about twelve or thirteen years old. The purport of this knocking was not thoroughly conceived, till the eldest child [claimed] to see the actual ghost of the deceased lady. When she had seen the ghost, a weak, ignorant publican also, who lived in the neighbourhood, asserted that he had seen it too; and Mr P—s himself, he also saw the ghost at the same time: the girl saw it without hands, in a shroud; the other two saw it with hands, all luminous and shining. There was one unlucky circumstance however in the apparition: though it appeared to several persons, and could knock, scratch, and flutter, yet its coming would have been to no manner of purpose, had it not been kindly assisted by the persons thus haunted. It was impossible for a ghost that could not speak, to make any [revelation]; the people therefore, to whom it appeared, kindly undertook to make the [revelation] themselves; and the ghost, by knocking, gave its assent to their methods of wording the accusation. When therefore the spirit taught the assistants, or rather the assistants had taught the spirit ... that Mr K— was the murderer, the road lay then open, and every night the farce was carried on, to the amusement of several, who attended with all the good-humour, which spending one night with novelty inspires; they jested with the ghost, soothed it, flattered it, while none was truly unhappy, but him whose character was thus rendered odious, and trifled with, merely to amuse idle curiosity.

To have a proper idea of this scene, as it is now carried on, the reader is to conceive a very small room with a bed in the middle, the girl at the usual hour of going to bed, is undressed and put in with proper solemnity; the spectators are next introduced, who sit looking at each other, suppressing laughter, and wait in silent expectation for the opening of the scene. As the ghost is a good deal offended at incredulity, the persons present are to conceal theirs, if they have any, as by this concealment they can only hope to gratify their curiosity. For, if they show ... a too prying, inquisitive, or ludicrous turn of thinking, the ghost continues usually silent. The spectators therefore have nothing for it, but to sit quiet and credulous, otherwise they must hear no ghost, which is no small disappointment to persons, who have come for no other purpose.

The girl who knows, by some secret, when the ghost is to appear, sometimes apprizes the assistants of its intended visitation. It first begins to scratch, and then to answer questions, giving two knocks for a negative, and one for an affirmative. By this means it tells whether a watch, when held up, be white, blue, yellow, or black; how many clergymen are in the room, though in this it is sometimes mistaken; it evidently distinguishes white men from negroes, with several other marks of sagacity; however, it is sometimes mistaken in questions of a private nature, when it deigns to answer them: for instance, the ghost called her father John instead of Thomas, a mistake indeed a little extraordinary in a ghost; but perhaps she was willing to verify the old proverb, that it is a wise child that knows its own father. However, though sometimes right, and sometimes wrong, she pretty invariably persists in one story, namely, that she was poisoned, in a cup of purl, by red arsenic, a poison unheard of before, by Mr K— in her last illness; and that she heartily wishes him hanged.

It is no easy matter to remark upon an evidence of this nature; but it may not be unnecessary to observe, that the ghost, though fond of company, is particularly modest upon these occasions, an enemy to the light of a candle, and almost always most silent before those, from whose rank and understanding she could most reasonably expect redress.

Here (pages 22–24), the author transcribes the overwhelmingly negative report of a committee of 'gentlemen of eminence for their rank, learning, and good sense' which was set up to investigate the phenomena. The committee's report concluded that 'it is the opinion of the whole of the assembly, that the child has some art of making or counterfeiting particular noises, and that there is no agency of higher cause'.

The question in this case, therefore, is not, whether the ghost be true or false, but who are the contrivers, or what can be the motives for this vile deception? But still it seems something extraordinary, how this imposition could be for so long carried on without a discovery. However [it] was the observation of Erasmus, that whenever people flock to see a miracle, they are generally sure of seeing a miracle; they bring an heated imagination, and an eager curiosity to the scene of the action, give themselves up blindly to deception, and each is better pleased with having it to say, that he had seen something very strange, than that he was made the dupe of his own credulity.

– Goldsmith (attrib.), *The Mystery Revealed*, pp. 2–28.

24
The Dog-Ghost of David Sutor

This extraordinary account is the third of three stories about 'Apparitions foretelling death' recorded in The Gentleman's Magazine *in 1731. The author explains that 'the following narrative, given by a gentleman of unexceptionable honour and veracity, has been lately published at Edinburgh'.*

The 'circumvallation' mentioned in the fourth paragraph is a military term for a protective rampart; it is not clear whether William Sutor built such a rampart or merely drew a circle round himself as was common when people wished to confront the spirits of the dead.

One William Sutor, aged about thirty-seven, a farmer in Middlemause (belonging to the Laird of Balgown, near Craighal), being about the month of December, 1728, in the fields with his servants, near his own house, overheard at some distance, as it were, an uncommon shrieking and noise; and they following the voice, fancied they saw a dark grey-coloured dog; but as it was a dark night, they concluded it was a fox, and accordingly were for setting on their dogs; but it was very observable that not one of [the dogs] would so much as point his head that way.

About a month after, the said Sutor being occasionally in the same spot, and much about the same time of night, it appeared to him again, and, in passing, touched him so smartly on the thigh, that he felt a pain all that night. In December, 1729, it again [came] up to him at about the same place, and passed him at some distance. In June, 1730, it appeared to him as formerly; and it was now he began to judge it was something extraordinary. On the last Monday of November, 1730, about sky-setting, as he was coming from Drumlochy, this officious visitor passed him as formerly, and in passing he distinctly heard it speak these words, 'Within eight or ten days, do or die;' and instantly disappeared, leaving him not a little perplexed.

Next morning he came to his brother James's house, and gave him a particular account of all that had happened. And that night, about ten o'clock, these two brothers, having been visiting their sister at Glanballow, and returning home, stept aside to see the remarkable spot, where they had no sooner arrived, than [the dog] appeared to William, who, pointing his finger to it, desired his brother and a servant, who was with them, to look to it; but neither of them could see any such thing.

Next Saturday evening, as William was at his sheepfold, it came up to him, and audibly uttered these words, 'Come to the spot of ground within half an hour.'

Whereupon he went home; and, taking a staff in his hand, came to the ground, being at last determined to see the issue. He had scarce encircled himself with a line of circumvallation when his troublesome familiar came up to him: he asked it, 'In the name of God, who are you?' It answered, 'I am David Sutor, George Sutor's brother. I killed a man more than thirty-five years ago at a bush by east the road as you go into the isle [sic].' He said to it, 'David Sutor was a man, and you appear as a dog.' It answered, 'I killed him with a dog, and am made to speak out of the mouth of a dog, and I tell you to go and bury these bones!'

This coming to the ears of the minister of Blair, the Lairds Glascloon and Rychalzie and about forty men, went together to the said isle; but after opening ground in several places, found no bones. On the second of December, about midnight, when William was in bed, the apparition came to his door, and said, 'Come away, you will find the bones at the side of the withered bush, and there are but eight left'; and told him at the same time for a sign that he would find the print of a cross impressed on the ground. Next day William and his brother, with about forty or fifty people who had convened out of curiosity, came to the place, where they discovered the bush and the cross by it; and upon digging the ground about a foot down found the eight bones; all which they immediately wrapped in clean linen, and, being put in a coffin with a mort-cloth over it, were interred that evening in the churchyard of Blair, attended by about a hundred persons.

Several persons in that county remember to have seen this David Sutor; and that he listed for a soldier and went abroad about thirty-four or thirty-five years ago.

– Gomme, *English Traditions and Foreign Customs*, pp. 194–95.

25
The Governor of Gibraltar's Wife

'Apparition at Tewing, Hertfordshire' is the heading George Laurence Gomme uses for this touching story about the wraith that appears to the Governor of Gibraltar at the moment of his wife's death.

General Joseph Sabine enjoyed a distinguished military and political career. He served during the Nine Years' War, the War of the Spanish Succession and at the Battle of Blenheim. In 1716 he became Commander of the British Army in Scotland, entered parliament in 1727 as Member for Berwick-on-Tweed, and became Governor of Gibraltar in 1730. He died at Gibraltar in October 1739.

Tewing (modern-day Tewin) lies between Welwyn Garden City and Stevenage and dates back to Anglo-Saxon times.

Dr Yarborough, the Rector of Tewing, Hertfordshire, who had a long and intimate acquaintance with the late General Sabine, Governor of Gibraltar, whose country seat was at Tewing, told me this story, which he had from the general's own mouth, who was a person of great honour and veracity, and much good sense.

That when he once lay dangerously ill of his wounds after a battle abroad, and began to recover, as he lay awake one night in his bed, having a candle in his chamber, he saw on the sudden the curtains drawn back at his bed's feet, and his wife, then in England (a lady whom he greatly loved), presenting herself to his full view, at the opening of the curtains, and then disappearing. He was amazed at the sight, and fell into deep reflections upon this extraordinary apparition. In a short time after he received the melancholy news from England that his beloved consort was dead, and that she died at such a time; which, as near as he could possibly recollect, was the very time on which he had seen that strange phenomenon.

This he immediately entered down in his notebook, continuing ever afterwards fully persuaded of the certainty of some apparitions, notwithstanding the general prejudice to the contrary; 'which,' said he often, 'I can from my own knowledge in this instance, confidently oppose upon the strongest grounds.'

This is the story, and I here set it down as I heard it from the above-mentioned worthy doctor, without making any remarks.

– Gomme, *English Traditions and Foreign Customs*, p. 184.

26
The Great Giant of Henllys

The contributor to The Athenaeum *who recounted the following story said it was still current along the banks of the River Wye at the time of writing (1847) though referring to events supposedly happening 'a century ago'. Strongly rooted in a sense of place – the two lakes mentioned in the story are both near the town of Rhayader, Powys – the storyteller observes that 'when related by the firelight during a winter's night in some solitary dwelling amongst the mountains, and the narration lengthened out by explanations and digressions, [it] produces an effect upon the listeners not to be soon effaced'.*

The contributor says he had first heard it fifty years previously and the story had never before appeared in print. It is remarkable, he says, for the accuracy and detail with which it portrays 'the method of exorcism among the Welsh'.

In some form or other, this legend continued to flourish in Wales and the Marches for many decades. Charlotte Burne's 'Roaring Bull of Bagbury' (see story no. 60), and Ella Leather's 'Black Vaughan', whose story is told in The Folklore of Herefordshire *of 1912 (pp. 29–30), are both plainly truncated variants of the same legend.*

About a century ago, there lived near the banks of the Wye a very wicked man, rich and extremely oppressive; who from his tyrannical conduct and the name of his residence was called *Y cawr mawr o'r Henllys* – the Great Giant of Henllys. After practising much oppression and tyranny in his neighbourhood, at length he died; and the country rejoiced exceedingly at this deliverance. But their joy was of short duration. Soon after his death, the country began to be troubled with strange disturbances. Fearful sounds were heard at night, and unaccountable appearances seen about the lonely parts of the roads and lanes – beginning with nightfall and increasing with the lateness of the hour; so that none but very courageous persons would venture out of doors ... For some time, the cause of these mysterious molestations greatly perplexed the country; but ere long, it was discovered that they were occasioned by the *cawr mawr o'r Henllys* –,who, in his ghostly state, and with his pristine malignity had come once more to trouble the neighbourhood. And then all peace of mind was gone. The women would not go to market, for fear of night overtaking them on their way home; and even the very horses started and trembled, and could scarcely be made to stir. Such was the state of things that all the country cried out for having this wicked spirit *laid*; and in accordance with this desire, three clergymen – some say, seven – undertook the work of exorcism. Having assembled in the parish church, in the dead of night, at the hour in which the spirit used to be most daring, and having drawn a circle round them on the floor in the vacant space before the altar, and each holding a lighted candle in his hand, they commenced their exorcisms. After reading [the requisite prayers and Bible readings] for some time, symptoms of the spirit's approach were perceived. He dashed forward from the other end of the church, in the form of a terrific monster; and with horrible roarings and bellowings, rushed towards them up the aisle, and sprang at them with his jaws extended. But the moment he reached the circle within which they stood, he fell back as from a stone wall, and instantly disappeared. So unexpected and appalling was the attack, that the candle of one of the exorcists went out – his faith not being sufficiently strong for such a trial.

However, they continued their adjurations; and the spirit again came forward in the same furious manner, in the form of a raging lion – and again met with the same repulse at the edge of the circle. Then again, as a monstrous bull – with the same result. He continued these assaults for a considerable time under different forms; – all of which are particularly described when the narration is complete.

At one time, he came up as a wave of the sea, foaming and threatening to overwhelm them, but dashing itself into spray and vanishing at the edge of the circle. At another time, it seemed as if the end of the church were falling to ruins on their heads with fearful crashing. During the course of these proceedings, so terrific was the scene that another candle went out – and even the remaining one burnt dim. But their faith returned – and their candles burnt brighter. So, they continued their exorcisms till at length the spirit appeared in his human form, as when living. They then spoke to him and asked him why he troubled the country; and he answered, 'I was bad when a man, I am worse now I am a devil' – and vanished in fire.

From this time forth, as they proceeded with their adjurations, the forms which he assumed became less and less terrific, and his manner less fierce – till at last he came in the form of a fly. When, they opened a tobacco-box, and, compelling him to enter it, they shut him in, and took him to Llyngwyn pool – some say Llynhilyn – and threw him in; there to remain for ninety-nine years – some say longer. At the expiration of that term he is to appear again, and be ten times worse than at first. So generally current is this story in the country, that some time ago, when persons were dragging one of these pools for eels, they were significantly cautioned not to disturb the tobacco-box and so release the *cawr* before his time!

– Anon., 'The Story of the Great Giant of Henllys',
The Athenaeum (28 August 1847), pp. 911–12.

27
The Haunted Chamber

In introducing this tale, the anonymous author observes that it was 'related in the Welsh language by an old man, who believed implicitly in its truth; and is here given without any alterations whatever, excepting such as are requisite in order to put an oral narration into a readable form.'

About the middle of the last century, there lived in one of the mountainous districts of Monmouthshire, called Blaenau Gwent, a pious and elderly dissenting minister by the name of Edmund Jones; who published a work upon ghosts and apparitions – in the existence of which he firmly believed. His wife – also a worthy and pious person – shared with him his belief in ghosts; but was possessed of greater courage, and did not evince the same dread of encountering them. About this time, there was in that neighbourhood an old mansion-house, a certain part of which had long been unoccupied, being haunted – especially one particular room, in which no one who knew the place could ever be persuaded to sleep; and such strangers as had, in a case of emergency, been put into it, could not remain there on account of the supernatural disturbances to which they were subject.

At length, Mrs Edmund Jones, having repeatedly heard of this, paid a visit to the house and requested to be allowed to pass the night in this apartment. The family at first remonstrated with her – and pointed out to her the unpleasant consequences of such a course; but as she persisted in her request, they ultimately determined to indulge her – and having made the necessary preparations for her accommodation, they showed her into the haunted room, and left her there with her candle lighted – retiring to rest. The old lady being thus left alone, locked her door; and, according to her usual custom, drew her chair to the table, and opening her Bible, began to read. Having continued in this manner a considerable time, in perfect silence and undisturbed, at the close of the passage which she was occupied in reading she chanced to raise her head from the book, and to look up; when she beheld standing before her, on the opposite side of the table, a form of terrific aspect, with his eyes fixed fiercely on her. She fixed her eyes on him in return, and gazed upon him in the most composed and unconcerned manner. After they had remained for some time looking at each other, the demon spoke, and said, 'Thy faith is in the candle.'

'Thou lyest,' said she; and taking the candle out of the candlestick, she turned it down and extinguished it in the socket. Then, in the triumph of her faith, she folded her arms, – and continued in her seat, setting at defiance the powers of darkness. Nor was she any more disturbed. From that time forth, the house never suffered from ghostly molestation.

– Anon., *The Athenaeum* (28 August 1847), p. 912.

28
The Haunting of Epworth Parsonage

'In 1716,' writes John Ingram, from whose account the narrative below is taken, 'the Rev. Samuel Wesley, father of the famous John Wesley, the founder of Methodism, was Rector of Epworth in Lincolnshire. During the months of December 1716, and January 1717, the parsonage was haunted in a most unpleasant fashion ... [This is] one of the best authenticated cases of haunted houses on record.'

Indeed no ghost story is better known than that of Old Jeffrey, the spirit so named by Emily Wesley, which disturbed the Rectory at Epworth. The authorities for the story are a statement and journal by the Revd Samuel Wesley written between 21 December 1716 and 1 January 1717, a series of family letters of 1717, a set of written statements made by witnesses to John Wesley in 1726, and a narrative composed many years after by John Wesley for The Arminian Magazine.

Ingram's account quotes the narrative published in the Arminian Magazine. *I have slightly abridged this very long story.*

'On December 2, 1716,' says John Wesley, 'while Robert Brown, my father's servant, was sitting with one of the maids, a little before ten at night, in the dining-room which opened into the garden, they both heard someone knocking at the door. Robert rose and opened it, but could see nobody. Quickly it knocked again and groaned. "It is Mr Turpine," said Robert, "he used to groan so." He opened the door again twice or thrice, the knocking being twice or thrice repeated; but still seeing nothing, and being a little startled, they rose up and went to bed. When Robert came to the top of the garret stairs, he saw a handmill, which was at a little distance, whirled about very swiftly. When he related this he said, "Nought vexed me but that it was empty. I thought if it had been but full of malt he might have ground his hand out for me." When he was in bed, he heard as it were the gobbling of a turkey-cock close to the bed-side, and soon after the sound of one stumbling over his shoes and boots; but there was none there, he had left them below. The next day he and the maid related these things to the other maid, who laughed heartily, and said, "What a couple of fools you are! I defy anything to fright me!" After churning in the evening, she put the butter in the tray, and had no sooner carried it into the dairy than she heard a knocking on the shelf where several puncheons of milk stood, first above the shelf, then below. She took the candle and searched both above and below, but, being able to find nothing, threw down butter, tray, and all, and ran away for life.

'The next evening, between five and six o'clock, my sister Molly, then about twenty years of age, sitting in the dining-room reading, heard as if it were the door that led into the hall open, and a person walking in that seemed to have on a silk nightgown, rustling and trailing along. It seemed to walk round her, and then to the door, then round again; but she could see nothing. She thought, "It signifies nothing to run away; for, whatever it is, it can run faster than me." So she rose, put her book under her arm, and walked slowly away. After supper, she was sitting with my sister Sukey (about a year older than her), in one of the chambers, and telling her what had happened. She made quite light of it, telling her, "I wonder you are so easily frightened. I would fain see what would frighten me." Presently a knocking began under the table. She took the candle and looked, but could find nothing. Then the iron casement began to clatter. Next the catch of the door moved up and down without ceasing. She started up, leaped into the bed without undressing, pulled the bed-clothes over her head, and never ventured to look up until next morning.

'A night or two after, my sister Hetty (a year younger than my sister Molly) was waiting as usual between nine and ten, to take away my father's candle, when she heard someone coming down the garret stairs, walking slowly by her, then going slowly down the best stairs, then up the back stairs and up the garret stairs, and at every step it seemed the house shook from top to bottom. Just then my father knocked, she went in, took his candle, and got to bed as fast as possible. In the morning she told it to my eldest sister, who told her, "You know I believe none of these things; pray let me take away the candle to-night, and I will find out the trick." She accordingly took my sister Hetty's place, and had no sooner taken away the candle, than she heard a noise below. She hastened down-stairs to the hall, where the noise was, but it was then in the kitchen. She ran into the kitchen, when it was drumming on the inside of the screen. When she went round it was drumming on the outside, and so always on the side opposite to her. Then she heard a knocking at the back kitchen door. She ran to it, unlocked it softly, and, when the knocking was repeated, suddenly opened it, but nothing was to be seen. As soon as she had shut it, the knocking began again. She opened it again, but could see nothing. When she went to shut the door, it was violently knocked against her; but she set her knee and her shoulder to the door, forced it to, and turned the key. Then the knocking began again; but she let it go on, and went up to bed. However, from that time she was thoroughly convinced that there was no imposture in the affair.

'The next morning, my sister telling my mother what had happened, she said, "If I hear anything myself, I shall know how to judge." Soon after she begged her mother to come into the nursery. She did, and heard, in the corner of the room, as it were the violent rocking of a cradle; but no cradle had been there for some years. She was convinced it was preternatural, and earnestly prayed it might not disturb her in her own chamber at the hours of retirement; and it never did. She now thought it was proper to tell my father. But he was extremely angry, and said, "Sukey, I am ashamed of you. These boys and girls frighten one another; but you are a woman of sense, and should know better. Let me hear of it no more."

'At six in the evening he had family prayers as usual. When he began the prayer for the King, a knocking began all round the room, and a thundering knock attended the Amen. The same was heard from this time every morning and evening while the prayer for the King was repeated. As both my father and mother are now at rest, and incapable of being pained thereby, I think it my duty to furnish the serious reader with a key to this circumstance.

'The year before King William died, my father observed my mother did not say Amen to the prayer for the King. She said she would not, for she did not believe the Prince of Orange was King. He vowed he would never cohabit with her until she did. He then took his horse and rode away, nor did she hear anything of him for a twelvemonth. He then came back and lived with her as before. But I fear his vow was not forgotten before God. [...]

'Being informed that Mr Hoole, the vicar of Haxey, could give me some further information, I walked over to him. He said ... "Robert Brown came over to me and told me your father desired my company; when I came, he gave me an account of all that had happened, particularly the knocking during family prayer. But that evening (to my great satisfaction) we heard no knocking at all. But between nine and ten a servant came in and said, "Old Jeffrey is coming (that was the name of one that had died in the house), for I hear the signal." This, they informed me, was heard every night about a quarter before ten. It was towards the top of the house, on the outside, at the north-east corner, resembling the loud creaking of a saw, or rather that of a windmill, when the body of it is turned about in order to shift the sails to the wind. We then heard a knocking over our heads, and Mr Wesley, catching up a candle, said, "Come, Sir, now you shall hear for yourself." We went up-stairs, he with much hope, and I (to say the truth) with much fear. When we came into the nursery, it was knocking in the next room: when we went there, it was knocking in the nursery; and there it continued to knock, though we came in, and particularly at the head of the bed (which was of wood) in which Miss Hetty and two of her younger sisters lay. Mr Wesley, observing that they were much affected, though asleep, sweating, and trembling exceeding, was very angry, and, pulling out a pistol, was going to fire at the place whence the sound came. But I snatched him by the arm and said, "Sir, you are convinced that this is something preternatural. If so, you cannot hurt it, but you give it power to hurt you." He then went close to the place and said, sternly: "Thou deaf and dumb devil! why dost thou fright these children who cannot answer for themselves? Come to me, in my study, that am a man!"

'Instantly it knocked his knock (the particular knock which he always used at the gate), as if it would shiver the board to pieces, and we heard nothing more that night.'

Commenting upon this portion of the narrative, as furnished by the Rev. Mr. Hoole, John Wesley remarks:

'Till this time my father had never heard the least disturbance in his study. But the next evening, as he attempted to go into his study (of which none had the key but himself), when he opened the door it was thrust back with such violence as had like to have thrown him down. However, he thrust the door open, and went in. Presently there was a knocking, first on one side, then on the other, and, after a time, in the next room, wherein my sister Nancy was. He went into that room, and, the noise continuing, adjured it to speak, but in vain. He then said, "These spirits love darkness: put out the candle, and perhaps it will speak." She did so, and he repeated the adjuration; but still there was only knocking, and no articulate sound. Upon this he said, "Nancy, two Christians are an overmatch for the devil. Go all of you down-stairs, it may be when I am alone he will have courage to speak." When she was gone, a thought came into his head, and he said, "If thou art the spirit of my son Samuel, I pray knock three knocks, and no more." Immediately all was silence, and there was no more knocking at all that night. I asked my sister Nancy (then fifteen years old), whether she was not afraid when my father used that adjuration. She answered she was sadly afraid it would speak when she put out the candle, but she was not at all afraid in the day-time, when it walked after her, only she thought when she was about her work, he might have done it for her and saved her the trouble. [...]

'By this time, all my sisters were so accustomed to these noises, that they gave them little disturbance. A gentle tapping at their bed-head usually began between nine and ten at night. They then commonly said to each other, "Jeffrey is coming; it is time to go to sleep." And if they heard a noise in the day, and said to my youngest sister, "Hark, Kezzy, Jeffrey is knocking above," she would run upstairs, and pursue it from room to room, saying she desired no better diversion. [...]

'My father and mother had just gone to bed and the candle was not taken away, when they heard three blows, and a second and a third three, as it were with a large oaken staff, struck upon a chest which stood by the bedside. My father immediately arose, put on his nightgown, and, hearing great noises below, took the candle and went down; my mother walked by his side. As they went down the broad stairs, they heard as if a vessel full of silver was poured upon my mother's breast and ran jingling down to her feet. Quickly after, there was a sound as if a large iron bell were thrown among many bottles under the stairs; but nothing was hurt. Soon after, our large mastiff dog came, and ran to shelter himself between them. While the disturbances continued he used to bark and leap, and snap on one side and the other, and that frequently before any person in the room heard any noise at all. But after two or three days he used to tremble, and creep away before the noise began. And by this the family knew it was at hand; nor did the observation ever fail. [...]

'Several gentlemen and clergymen now earnestly advised my father to quit the house. But he constantly answered, "No: let the devil flee from me; I will never flee from the devil." But he wrote to my eldest brother, at London, to come down. He was preparing so to do, when another letter came informing him the disturbances were over, after they had continued (the latter part of the time day and night), from the 2nd of December to the end of January. [...]

'No satisfactory explanation of these remarkable circumstances has ever, so far as we can discover, been afforded.'

– Ingram, *Haunted Homes and Family Traditions of Great Britain*, pp. 83–94.

29
Lord Lyttelton's Warning

'Sir,' said Dr Johnson (so Andrew Lang writes in The Book of Dreams and Ghosts, *1897), 'it is the most extraordinary thing that has happened in my day.'*

Lang points out that 'the doctor's day included the rising of 1745 and of the Wesleyans, the seizure of Canada, the Seven Years' War, the American Rebellion, the Cock Lane ghost, and other singular occurrences, but "the most extraordinary thing" was – Lord Lyttelton's ghost! Famous as is that spectre, nobody knows what it was, nor even whether there was any spectre at all'.

'Thomas, Lord Lyttelton,' Lang continues, 'was born in 1744. In 1768 he entered the House of Commons. In 1769 he was unseated for bribery. He then vanishes from public view, probably he was playing the prodigal at home and abroad, till February, 1772, when he returned to his father's house, and married. He then went abroad (with a barmaid) till 1773, when his father died. In January, 1774, he took his seat in the House of Lords. In November 1779 Lyttelton went into Opposition. On Thursday, 25th November, he denounced the Government in a magnificent speech. As to a sinecure which he held, he said, "Perhaps I shall not keep it long!" Something had happened!'

The story of the warning received by Lord Lyttelton (or Lyttleton) has been widely anthologised since it was first the talk of the town, and details often vary from compilation to compilation. This version comes from an 1816 issue of The Gentleman's Magazine *and is presented under the heading 'Instances of Maniacal Delusion Exemplified'. Interestingly, Lord Lyttelton here is described, not as a profligate, but as a refined man of learning: neither is there any suggestion – as there is for instance in John Ingram's account in* Haunted Homes and Family Traditions of Great Britain *– that the apparition was of a woman he had wronged and who had recently died from a broken heart.*

The death of the celebrated and erudite Thomas, Lord Lyttelton, from the singularity of the circumstances attending it, cannot fail to live in the memory of those who have heard it. He professed to have been warned of his death, and the time thereof, as follows: About a week before he died, he said, he went to bed pretty well, but restless. Soon after his servant had left him, he heard a footstep, at the bottom of his bed. He raised himself, in order to see what it could be, when one of the most angelic female figures that imagination could possibly paint presented itself before him, and with a commanding voice and action, bade him attend and prepare himself, for on such a night, and at the hour of twelve, he would surely die! He attempted to address the vision, but was unable; and the ghost vanished, and left him in a state more easily conceived than could be described. His valet found him in the morning more dead than alive; and it was some hours before his Lordship could be recovered sufficiently to send for his friends, to whom he thought it necessary to communicate this extraordinary circumstance. Mr Miles Peter Andrews was one of the number sent for, being at that time one of his most intimate associates. Every person to whom Lord Lyttelton told the tale naturally turned it into ridicule, all knowing him to be very nervous and superstitious, and tried to make him believe it was a dream, as they certainly considered so themselves.

Mr M. P. Andrews had business which called him to Dartford, and therefore soon took his leave, thinking Lord Lyttelton quite composed on this subject, so that his friend's dream dwelt so little on his imagination, that he did not even recollect the time when it was predicted that the event would take place [...] till, about four o'clock the [next] day, an express arrived to inform him of Lord Lyttelton's death, and the manner of it, by a friend who was present, and gave the following particular account of it: That, on the morning before Lord Lyttelton died, he entered the breakfast-room between ten and eleven o'clock; appeared rather thoughtful, and did not answer any inquiries made by his friends respecting his health, etc. At dinner he seemed much better, and when the cloth was taken away, he exclaimed, 'Richard's himself again!' But as night came on the gloom of the morning returned. However, as this was the predicted night of dissolution, his friends agreed that it would be right to alter the clocks and watches in the house. This was managed by the steward, without Lord Lyttelton suspecting anything of it; his own watch, which lay on his dressing-table, being altered by his valet.

During the evening they got him into some pleasant discussions, in which he distinguished himself with peculiar wit and pleasantry. At half after eleven, as he conceived it, from the alteration of the clocks (but it was only eleven), he said he was tired, and would retire to bed; bid them a good-night, and left them all delighted with his calm appearance. During the day not the least hint was given by anyone to him of the dream; but of course, as soon as he had withdrawn, the conversation instantly turned upon it. The discourse continued till nearly twelve o'clock, when the door being hastily opened, Lord Lyttelton's valet entered, pale as death, crying out, 'My Lord is dying!' His friends flew to his bedside, but he expired before they could all assemble round him! Lord Lyttelton's valet gave to them the following statement: 'That Lord Lyttelton made his usual preparations for bed; that he kept every now and then looking at his watch; that when he got into bed, he ordered his curtains to be closed at the foot. It was now within a minute or two of twelve by his watch; he asked to look at mine, and seemed pleased to find it nearly keep time with his own. His Lordship then put them both to his ear, to satisfy himself if they went. When it was more than a quarter after twelve by our watches, he said, "This mysterious lady is not a true prophetess, I find." When it was near the real hour of twelve, he said, "Come, I'll wait no longer. Get me my medicine; I'll take it, and try to sleep!" I just stepped into the dressing-room to prepare the physic, and had mixed it, when I thought I heard my Lord breathing very hard. I ran to him, and found him in the agonies of death.'

– Gomme, *English Traditions and Foreign Customs*, pp. 97–99.

30
The Murder of Sergeant Davies

In 1831, Sir Walter Scott wrote an essay for the 'Bannatyne Club' in which he recounted several cases where evidence provided by a ghost was brought to court in a trial for murder, and focused in particular on the case of the death of Sergeant Davies in or around Glenshee about three years after the Battle of Culloden.

The first of the accounts below is taken from Scott's article. The second is an extract from Andrew Lang's discussion of Scott's essay, and fills in some of the detail.

Sergeant Davies 1

It was about three years after the battle of Culloden that this poor man, Sergeant Davies, was quartered, with a small military party, in an uncommonly wild part of the Highlands, near the country of the Farquharsons, as it is called, and adjacent to that which is now the property of the Earl of Fife. A more waste tract of mountain and bog, rocks and ravines, extending from Dubrach to Glenshee, without habitations of any kind until you reach Glenclunie, is scarce to be met with in Scotland. A more fit locality, therefore, for a deed of murder, could hardly be pointed out, nor one which could tend more to agitate superstitious feelings. The hill of Christie, on which the murder was actually committed, is a local name, which is probably known in the country, though the Editor [Scott] has been unable to discover it more specially, but it certainly forms part of the ridge to which the general description applies. Davies was attached to the country where he had his residence, by the great plenty of sport which it afforded, and, when dispatched upon duty across these mountains, he usually went at some distance from his men, and followed his game without regarding the hints thrown out about danger from the country people. To this he was exposed, not only from his being intrusted with the odious office of depriving the people of their arms and national dress, but still more from his usually carrying about with him a stock of money and valuables, considerable for the time and period, and enough of itself to be a temptation to his murder.

On the 28th day of September, the Sergeant set forth, along with a party, which was to communicate with a separate party of English soldiers at Glenshee; but when Davies's men came to the place of rendezvous, their commander was not with them, and the privates could only say that they had heard the report of his gun after he had parted from them on his solitary sport. In short, Sergeant Arthur Davies was seen no more in this life, and his remains were long sought for in vain. At length a native of the country, named M'Pherson, made it known to more than one person that the spirit of the unfortunate huntsman had appeared to him, and told him he had been murdered by two Highlanders, natives of the country, named Duncan Terig alias Clerk, and Alexander Bane Macdonald. Proofs accumulated, and a person was even found to bear witness, that lying in concealment upon the hill of Christie, the spot where poor Davies was killed, he and another man, now dead, saw the crime committed with their own eyes. A girl whom Clerk afterwards married, was, nearly at the same time, seen in possession of two valuable rings which the Sergeant used to have about his person. Lastly, the counsel and agent of the prisoners were convinced of their guilt. Yet, notwithstanding all these suspicious circumstances, the panels were ultimately acquitted by the jury.

This was chiefly owing to the ridicule thrown upon the story by the incident of the ghost, which was enhanced seemingly, if not in reality, by the ghost-seer stating the spirit to have spoken as good Gaelic as he had ever heard in Lochaber. – 'Pretty well,' answered Mr M'Intosh, 'for the ghost of an English sergeant!' This was indeed no sound jest, for there was nothing more ridiculous, in a ghost speaking a language which he did not understand when in the body, than there was in his appearing at all. But still the counsel had a right to seize upon whatever could benefit his clients, and there is no doubt that this observation rendered the evidence of the spectre yet more ridiculous. In short, it is probable that the ghost of Sergeant Davies, had he actually been to devise how to prevent these two men from being executed for his own murder, could hardly have contrived a better mode than by the apparition in the manner which was sworn to.

The most rational supposition seems to be, that the crime had come to M'Pherson, the ghost-seer's knowledge, by ordinary means, of which there is some evidence, but desiring to have a reason for communicating it, which could not be objected to by the people of the country, he had invented this machinery of the ghost, whose commands, according to Highland belief, were not to be disobeyed. If such were his motives, his legend, though it seemed to set his own tongue at liberty upon the subject, yet it impressed on his evidence the fate of Cassandra's prophecies, that, however true, it should not have the fortune to be believed.

ABBOTSFORD, 18 March, 1830.

– Scott, 'The Trial of Duncan Terig, alias Clerk, and Alexander Bain Macdonald for the Murder of Arthur Davies, Sergeant in General Guise's Regiment of Foot, June MDCC.LIV' online document.

Sergeant Davies 2

Macpherson declared that he had seen an apparition of a man in blue, who said, 'I am Sergeant Davies,' that he at first took this man for a brother of Donald Farquharson's, that he followed the man, or phantasm, to the door, where the spectre repeated its assertions, and pointed out the spot where the bones lay. He found them, and then went, as already shown, to Donald Farquharson. Between the first vision and the burying, the ghost came to him naked, and this led him to inter the remains. On the second appearance, the ghost denounced the prisoners. Macpherson gave other evidence, not spectral, which implicated Clerk [...] Macpherson added that he told his tale to none of the people with him in the sheiling, but that Isobel McHardie assured him she 'saw such a vision'. Isobel, in whose service Macpherson had been, deponed that, while she lay at one end of the sheiling and Macpherson at the other, 'she saw something naked come in at the door, which frighted her so much that she drew the clothes over her head.' Next day she asked Macpherson what it was, and he replied 'she might be easy, for that it would not trouble them any more.'

– Lang, *Cock Lane and Common Sense*, pp. 255–58.

31
'Oh, Dear Son, Thee Art Dead!'

This story is represented as the personal experience of a dissenting minister, 'the late Joseph Wilkins', who dates the events to 1754.

Being one night asleep [Joseph Wilkins] dreamed he was travelling to London, and that, as it would not be much out of his way, he would go by Gloucestershire and call upon his friends. Accordingly he arrived at his father's house, but, finding the front door closed, he went round to the back and there entered. The family, however, being already in bed, he ascended the stairs and entered his father's bedchamber. Him he found asleep; but to his mother, who was awake, he said, as he walked round to her side of the bed, 'Mother, I am going on a long journey, and am come to bid you good-bye'; to which she answered, 'Oh, dear son, thee art dead!' Though struck with the distinctness of the dream, Mr Wilkins attached no importance to it, till, to his surprise, a letter arrived from his father, addressed to himself, if alive – or, if not, to his surviving friends – begging earnestly for immediate intelligence, since they were under great apprehensions that their son was either dead, or in danger of death; for that, on such a night (naming that on which the above dream had occurred), he, the father, being asleep, and Mrs Wilkins awake, she had distinctly heard somebody try to open the fore-door, which being fast, the person had gone round to the back and there entered. She perfectly recognised the footstep to be that of her son, who had ascended the stairs, and entering the bedchamber, had said to her, 'Mother, I am going on a long journey, and am come to wish you good-bye'; whereupon she had answered, 'Oh, dear son, thee art dead!' Much alarmed, she had awakened her husband and related what had occurred, assuring him that it was not a dream, for that she had not been asleep at all. Mr Wilkins mentions that he had frequently discussed the subject with his mother, on whom the impression made was even stronger than on himself. Neither death nor anything else remarkable ensued.

– Crowe, *The Night-Side of Nature*, pp. 103–04.

32
Old Coles

This eighteenth-century tale was one of a selection of stories of haunting contributed in 1855 to The Gentleman's Magazine *by J. Noake.*

Leigh Court Barn, through which the spectre was supposed to have driven with his coach and four, lies between Worcester and Hereford, and was built in 1344 as a tithe barn for Pershore Abbey. It is 46 metres long; its roof is supported by eighteen cruck blades, each made from a single oak tree. In the care now of English Heritage, it is the largest cruck construction in Britain and is open to the public during the summer months.

At Leigh a spectre known as 'Old Coles' formerly appeared; and at dead of night would drive a coach and four down a part of the road, dash [through] the great barn at Leigh Court, and then cool the fiery nostrils of his steeds in the waters of the Teme ... [T]his perturbed spirit was at length laid in a neighbouring pool by twelve parsons, at twelve at night, by the light of an inch of candle; and as he was not to rise again until the candle was quite burnt out, it was therefore thrown into the pool, and to make all sure, the pool was filled up;

'And peaceful ever after slept
Old Coles's shade.'

– Gomme, *English Traditions and Foreign Customs*, p. 209.

33
Parson Dodge and the Spectral Coach

According to legend, Cornwall has been particularly fortunate in the number of ghost-layers who have lived there – not only John Ruddle whose laying of the ghost of Dorothy Dingley is story no. 7 in this collection, but also Parson Flavell, Parson Corker, Parson Woods and Parson Jago. Nevertheless, perhaps the most famous Cornish ghost-layer of all is Parson Dodge of Talland.

The Revd Richard Dodge was vicar of Talland, a coastal village between Looe and Polperro in Cornwall, from 1713 till his death in 1746 in his ninety-third year. By all accounts he was a very singular man, feared and revered in almost equal amounts for his ability to drive out evil spirits, and suspected, too, of being in league with local smugglers. A footnote in Robert Hunt's Popular Romances of the West of England *(p. 230) quotes Thomas Bond's* Topographical and Historical Sketches of the Boroughs of East and West Looe *(1823) as follows: 'He had the reputation of being deeply skilled in the black arts and would raise ghosts, or send them into the Dead Sea, at the nod of his head. The common people, not only in his own parish, but throughout the neighbourhood, stood in the greatest awe of him, and to meet him on the highway at midnight produced the utmost horror; he was then driving out the evil spirits; many of them were seen, in all sorts of shapes, flying and running before him, and he pursuing them with his whip in a most daring manner ...'*

The most familiar and often quoted account of his encounter with the spectral coach is that contributed to Romances of the West of England *by Dr Thomas Quiller Couch (son of the eminent naturalist Jonathan Couch and father of Sir Arthur Quiller-Couch, literary lion of the early twentieth century). Quiller Couch also published the story as an addendum to his father's* History of Polperro, *which he caused to be published posthumously in 1871. The two versions are substantially the same except for the regularising of the English in the Hunt version, and the odd fact that the name of the vicar who shared Parson Dodge's adventure undergoes a change between the two versions. In* The History of Polperro *Quiller Couch calls him Richard Grylls (see below) and in* Popular Romances of the West of England *he calls him Abraham Mills. There is detective work here for those so-minded. I cannot discover whether there was a Revd Richard Grylls in Lanreath in the early eighteenth century, but a Jeremiah Mills and later an Isaac Mills were vicars of St Cuby's in the adjoining parish of Duloe from 1704 till 1767.*

The Duloe connection is strengthened by the fact that this parish also has a Parson Dodge story. 'A similar, and possibly the same story,' an information leaflet at Talland says, 'is told in Duloe parish where there is a tradition that on dark and stormy nights the ghost of Sir John Anstis, Garter King of Arms, can be seen driving from his house at Westnorth to Tremadart in a coach drawn by six headless coal-black horses. Once twelve clergymen met at midnight near Tremadart to try and lay this ghost but they failed. It is said that finally Doige [sic] was called in and he banished the ghost to Blackdown for a thousand years and said it should be no larger than a mouse.'

The reference to shrinking the ghost to the size of a mouse is another puzzle. This motif does not appear in either of Quiller Couch's versions of the story (or anywhere else that I have so far found) but, under the heading 'GHOST BUSTER', one of the display boards at Talland mentions Parson Dodge and says: 'On one occasion he was called in to help with a coachman driving a team of headless horses that had been terrorizing the area between Lanreath and Duloe. He is said to have shrunk him to the size of a mouse. So do be careful if you drive across the area known as Blackadon (between Lanreath and Duloe), don't drive over any little creatures that cross your path as it may be the coachman and his team of headless horses!!!' It makes no mention of where this bit of folklore comes from.

Further references: a ballad, 'The Talland Ghost Hunter', written and sung by John Langford can be heard on YouTube at www.youtube.com/watch?v=MjnCJKM4jsk.

The old vicarage-house at Talland, as seen from the Looe road; its low roof and grey walls peeping prettily from between the dense boughs of ash and elm that environed it was as picturesque an object as you could wish to see. The seclusion of its situation was enhanced by the character of the house itself. It was an odd-looking, old-fashioned building, erected apparently in an age when asceticism and self-denial were more in vogue than at present, with a stern disregard of the comfort of the inhabitant, and in utter ignorance or contempt of received principles of taste. As if not secure enough in its retirement, a high wall enclosing a courtlage in front, effectually protected its inmates from the passing wayfarer, and only revealed the upper part of the house, with its small gothic windows, slated roofs, and heavy chimneys, partly hidden by the evergreen shrubs which grew in the enclosure. Such was it until its removal a few years since, and such was it as it lay sweetly in the shadows of an autumnal evening one hundred and thirty years ago, when a stranger in the garb of a country labourer knocked at the wicket gate which conducted to the court. After a little delay a servant-girl appeared, and finding that the countryman bore a message to the vicar, admitted him within the walls, and conducted him along a paved passage to the little, low, damp parlour where sat the good man. The Rev. Mr Dodge, to whom the messenger was thus introduced, was in many respects a remarkable man, and you would instantly have judged as much of him as he sat before the fire in his high-back chair in an attitude of thought, arranging, perhaps, the heads of his next sabbath's discourse. His heavy eyebrows, throwing into shade his serious eyes, and, indeed the whole contour of his face marked him as a man of great firmness of character, and of much moral and personal courage. His suit of sober black, and full bottomed periwig also added to his dignity, and gave him an appearance of greater age than he was entitled to, for he was then only verging on sixty. The time and the place gave him abundant exercise for his valour and decision, for many of his parishioners got their living by the contraband trade, and were too often men of great daring, and very unscrupulous; little likely to bear with patience reflections on the dishonesty of their calling. Nevertheless the vicar was fearless in reprehending it, and his frank exhortations were at least quietly listened to on account of the simple honesty of the man, and his well-known kindness of heart. The eccentricity of his life, too, had a wonderful effect in procuring him the respect, not to say the awe of a superstitious race. Ghosts in those day had more freedom accorded them, or had more business with the visible world than at present; and the parson was frequently required by his parishioners to draw from the uneasy spirit the dread secret which troubled it, or by the aid of the solemn prayers of the church to set it at rest for ever. Our parson had a fame as an exorcist which was not confined to the bounds of his parish, nor limited to the age in which he lived.

'Well, my good man, what brings you hither?' said the clergyman to the messenger.

'A letter, please your reverence, from Mr Grylls of Lanreath,' answered the countryman, handing him a letter.

Mr Dodge opened it, and read as follows:-

My DEAR BROTHER DODGE,

I have ventured to trouble you, at the earnest request of the people of my parish, with a matter of which some particulars have, doubtless, reached you, and which has caused, and is causing much terror in my neighbourhood. For its fuller explication, I will be so tedious as to recount to you the whole of this strange story as it has reached my ears, for as yet I have not satisfied my eyes of its truth. It has been told me by men of honest and good report, (witnesses of what they relate), with such strong assurances, that it behoves us to look more closely into the matter. There is in this neighbourhood a barren bit of moor which had no owner, or rather more than one, for the lords of the adjoining manors debated its ownership between themselves, and both determined to take it from the poor, who have, time without mind, regarded it as common. And truly it is little to the credit of these gentlemen, that they should strive for a thing so worthless as scarce to bear the cost of law, and yet of no mean value to poor labouring people. The two litigants, however, contested it with as much violence as if it had been a field of great price and especially one, an old man, whose thoughts should have been less set on possessions he was soon to leave, had so set his heart on the success of his suit, that the loss of it a few years back is said to have much hastened his death. Nor, indeed, after death, if current reports are worthy of credit, does he quit his claim to it; for at night-time his apparition is seen on the moor to the great fright of the neighbouring villagers. A public path leads by at no great distance from the spot, and on divers occasions has the labourer returning from his work been scared nigh unto lunacy by sights and sounds of a very dreadful character. The appearance is said to be that of a man habited in black, driving a carriage drawn by headless horses. This is, I avow, very marvellous to believe, but it has had so much credible testimony in my parish that some steps seem necessary to allay the excitement it causes. I have been applied to for this purpose, and my present business is to ask your assistance in the matter, either to quiet the minds of the country people if it be only a simple terror; or if there be truth in it, to set the troubled spirit of the man at rest. My messenger who is a hard-working, trustworthy man, will give you more information if it be needed, for, from report he is acquainted with most of the circumstances, and will bring back your advice, and, I trust, promise of assistance.

Not doubting of your help herein, I do with my very hearty commendation commit you to God's protection and blessing, and am,

Your very loving Brother,

R. GRYLLS.

This remarkable letter was read and re-read while the countryman sat watching its effect on the parson's countenance, in surprise that it changed but little from its usual sedate and settled character. Turning at length to the man, Mr Dodge inquired, 'Are you then acquainted with my good friend Grylls?'

'Loft to know en, Zur,' replied the messenger, 'considerin I've bin sex'on o' the parish for vourteen years, and that me and my fam'ly have been much beholden to the kindness of the Rector both in sickness and health.'

'You are also not without some knowledge of the things related in this letter. Have you been an eye-witness to any of those strange sights?'

'As var as I'm consarned, Sir, I've been 'pon the road all hours, night and day and I can zay that I never zeed anything wus than myzelf. Wan night, tes true my wife and I were awoke by the rattle of wheels, which was also heered by some of our neighbours, and we all consider'd that it must be the black coach. But, law, Sir! we have every day such stories told o'n by creditable people that 'tisn't vur me, a poor plain, ignorant man to doubt et.'

'And how far is the moor from Lanreath?'

'About two miles, and please your reverance. The whole parish is so frightened that vew will venture far after dummut, vut et hath o' late come much nigher the church-town. A man who is esteemed a pious and sensible man by many, though belonging to the Anabaptists, as they be called, went a few weeks agone to the moor, ('tis called Blackadon), at midnight vur to lay the sperrit; hes neighbours all axed en to do et; and he was so frightened at what he zeed that he'th bin nearly mazed ever since [...] Most voks believe, as rightly they shud, what hath so many witnesses, though there be zome, young chaps, chiefly, who think they knuw more than their vaathers who won't hear o't though it be sworn to 'pon the Book.'

'If those things are disbelieved, friend, and without inquiry, which your disbeliever is ever the first to shirk, of what use is human testimony on any matter? That ghosts have returned to the earth, either for the discovery of murder, or to make restitution for other injustice committed in the flesh, or compelled thereto by the incantations of sorcery, or to communicate tidings from another world, has been testified to in all ages, and many are the instances which have been left to us both in sacred and profane authors. Did not Brutus, when in Asia, as is related by Plutarch see – '

Just at this moment the parson's handmaid said that a person with a hasty message waited on him in the kitchen, or the parson would probably have detailed all those cases in history general and biblical with which his reading had acquainted him; not much we fear to the comfort and edification of the sexton who had to return to Lanreath, a long and dreary road after nightfall. So instead, he directed the girl to take the man with her to the kitchen, and to give him such refreshment as he needed. Meanwhile he wrote to Mr Grylls telling him that on the next day he had to visit some sick persons in the parish and could not come, but that on the following evening he should be ready to proceed with him to the moor.

On the night appointed the two clergymen left the Lanreath rectory on horseback and reached the moor at ten o'clock. Bleak and dismal did it look by day, but then there was the distant landscape dotted over with pretty homesteads to relieve its desolation. Now, nothing was to be seen but the black patch of sterile moor on which they stood, nothing heard but the wind as it swept in gusts across the bare hill, and howled dismally through a stunted grove of trees that grew in a glen below them, except the occasional baying of dogs from the farm-houses in the distance ... Slowly and dismally passed the time as they conversed, and anon stopped to look and listen for the approach of their ghostly visitor. In vain. Though the night was as dark and murky as a ghost could wish, the coach and its driver came not.

After a considerable stay, the two clergymen consulted together, and determined that it was useless to watch any longer for that night, but that they would meet on some other, when perhaps, it might please his ghostship to appear. Accordingly, with a few words of leave-taking, they separated, Mr Grylls for the rectory and Mr Dodge, by a short cut across the moor which shortened his journey by half a mile, for the vicarage of Talland.

The vicar rode on at an ambling pace which his good mare sustained without urging until at the bottom of a valley not far from Blackadon the animal became very uneasy, pricked up her ears, snorted, and moved from side to side of the road as if something stood in the path before her. The parson tightened the reins, and applied whip and spur to her sides, but the horse usually docile, became very unruly, made several attempts to turn, and when prevented threw herself upon her haunches. Whip and spur were applied again and again, to no other purpose than to add to the horse's terror. To the rider nothing was apparent which could account for the sudden restiveness of his beast. He dismounted and attempted in turns to lead or drag her, but both were impossible and attended with no small risk of snapping the reins. She was remounted with great difficulty, and yet another unsuccessful attempt made to urge her forward. At length Parson Dodge, judging it to be some special signal from Heaven which it would be dangerous to neglect, threw the reins on the neck of his steed, which wheeling round, started backwards in a direction towards the moor, at a pace which rendered the rider's seat neither a pleasant nor a safe one. In an astonishingly short space of time they were once more on Blackadon.

By this time the bare outline of the moor was broken by a large black group of objects which the darkness prevented Dodge from defining. On approaching this unaccountable appearance the mare was seized with fresh fury, and it was with great difficulty that she could be brought to face this new cause of fright. In the pauses of the mare's prancing the vicar discovered to his horror the much dreaded spectacle of the black coach with its headless steeds, and terrible to relate, his friend, Mr Grylls, lying prostrate on the ground before the sable driver. Little time was left to him call up his courage for this fearful emergency; for just as the vicar begun to give utterance to the earnest prayer which struggled to his lips, the spectre shouted 'Dodge is come! I must be gone!' and forthwith leaped into his chariot, and disappeared across the moor.

The fury of the mare now subsided, and Dodge was enabled to approach his friend who was lying motionless and speechless, with his face buried in the heather.

Meanwhile the rector's horse, which had taken fright at the apparition, and had thrown his rider to the ground on or near the spot where he was found lying, made homeward at a furious speed, and stopped not until he had reached his stable door. The sound of his hoofs as he galloped madly through the village awoke the cottagers, most of whom had been some hours in their beds. Many eager faces, staring with affright, thronged round the rectory, and added by their various conjectures to the fright and apprehensions of the family.

The villagers, gathering courage as their numbers increased, agreed to go in search of the missing clergyman, and started off in a compact body, a few on horseback, but the greater number on foot, in the direction of Blackadon. Here they discovered their rector in the arms of Parson Dodge, and recovered so far as to be able to speak. Still there was a wildness in his eye, and an incoherency in his speech, that showed that his reason was, at least, temporarily unsettled by the fright. In this condition he was taken to his home, followed by his reverend companion.

Here ended this strange adventure; for Mr Grylls quickly regained his reason, Parson Dodge got safely back to Talland, and from that time to this nothing has been heard or seen of the black ghost or his chariot.

– Couch, *The History of Polperro*, pp. 86–91.

34
A Very Dangerous Rabbit

The Cornish village of Egloshayle lies on the estuary of the River Camel opposite Wadebridge. Its name derives from the old Cornish language – 'eglos', *meaning church and* 'heyl', *meaning estuary. Egloshayle was a settlement in the Bronze Age and at a later date a river port.*

A road and a low wall separate the Parish church of St Peter from the marshes. A handsome and gloomy building in the Perpendicular Gothic style, St Peter's has a Norman font, a stone pulpit from the fifteenth century, a ring of eight bells and a lichen-covered stone plaque set into the wall near the porch announcing that 'whoever is seen loitering in the churchyard or behaving indecently in the church during DIVINE SERVICE will be prosecuted according to law'. Advice that maybe the young man who features in this legend should have heeded! An information sheet in the church (written in French, Italian and Spanish) says that legend has it that the churchyard is haunted by a white rabbit.

The local-interest writer whose account I quote here sets the scene thus: 'This valley of the Camel is full of haunted lanes and houses. A mile or so up the river stands the ancient church of Egloshayle. Under a night sky the church is scarcely visible. But if the clouds roll back from the moon, and let a sudden blaze of light fall over the river bed, you will see the old grey tower clearly, standing out from a group of chestnut trees, and may even discern an open space beside the churchyard wall where the high road meets the lane leading to the village. The road gleams beneath the moonlight; but you are too far distant to see any object moving on it.'

Then the story begins:

If it were otherwise, you might now see – but never save when the moon is bright – a white rabbit gambolling about this open space beside the churchyard wall; a pretty, long-eared rabbit with pink eyes, like any child's pet escaped from its hutch. It goes loppeting about among the grasses by the corner of the marsh:– and if any one should pass, will sit and look at him with fearless eyes. And well it may. It has nothing to dread from any one dwelling in those parts. No villager would attempt to catch it. No boy would aim a blow at it. If any one walking late sees the white rabbit lopping at his heels, he makes no effort to drive it away, but quickens his pace, and hopes some good angel may stand between him and harm. A belated postman, terrified to find he could not shake off the pretty white creature at his heels, lost his head and turned and struck fiercely at it with his oaken cudgel. He felt the stick fall on the soft back of the rabbit, such a blow as might have killed a much larger animal. But the rabbit lopped on as if nothing had happened. The cudgel it was which was broken – shivered into splinters, as if it had struck upon a rock.

No one can tell the history of the rabbit; but our grandfathers knew and feared it as we do ourselves, and it was in their time that the last deliberate effort to meddle with the creature took place. The attempt was made by a stranger, and it happened in this wise. A number of young men were drinking together in the bar-room of the chief inn of the town. As the evening wore away, the talk grew high; and, at last, when all the party were heated, somebody spoke of the white rabbit. Instantly the stranger began to jeer a silly story such as that would never be believed outside a poky country town where nobody had anything better to do than to listen to the first idle tale told him. What harm could a rabbit do anybody? He would like nothing better than to shoot it.

One of the others drew aside the shutter and looked out. The street was as bright as day, and overhead they could see the full moon sailing, free of clouds. 'Tha'd best go now,' he said. 'When the moon shines like this, tha'll find the rabbit by the church.'

A gun was hanging on the wall. It was taken down and loaded amid a babble of jeers and angry retorts; and then the party crowded to the door to watch the stranger stride down the moonlit street, whistling merrily as he went. They saw him pass upon the bridge, and then went back to their bottles.

But some strange feeling of uneasiness had settled over them. Not one seemed inclined to sit down again. They moved restlessly about the room, and presently one of them went to the door and looked out. The others asked eagerly if he heard anything, though they knew the stranger could not have reached the church: and then one suggested that it was a shame to allow a man who had no knowledge of his danger to encounter it alone. The others agreed as readily as men will when they have done what does not please them, and without more delay they set off in a body. They trudged along saying nothing; but when they came near the church, they heard a report and a loud cry; and, with one accord, they ran to the open space with beating hearts. Neither man nor rabbit was to be seen. They ran up and down calling his name; there was no reply. He was not in the lane, nor on the high road, nor on the marsh, where, under the bright moonlight, the motion of a water hen could have been seen with ease. At last one of the searchers leapt up on the churchyard wall, and sprang down on the inner side, calling on his friends to follow him. There they found him lying dead, with one barrel of his gun discharged and the contents buried in his body. That happened many years ago; but still the stranger may be seen leaning over the low wall, pointing an ancient flint-lock gun at some object which moves quickly in the long grass.

– Norway, *Highways and Byways of Devon and Cornwall*, pp. 336–38.

35
The Wynyard Wraith

This story of the appearance of a young man to his brother at the moment of his death has been included in many anthologies of ghost stories from the beginning of the nineteenth century through to modern times. The present account has been taken from Frederick George Lee's The Other World. *Lee points out that it is unusual in that the wraith appears in broad daylight and is seen by more than one person, both of whom believe they have in real truth seen the ghost of Wynyard's brother.*

Lee adds several pieces of information, which indicate how extensively this story was discussed and for how long. He tells the reader that the record of this came to him through a friend and that another acquaintance had told him that he had made enquiries among the Wynyard family and they had told him that they had 'each heard it from [George Wynyard's] own mouth'. This correspondent also told him that 'a gentleman, whose accuracy of recollection exceeds that of most people, had told [him] that he had heard the late Sir John Sherbroke, the other party in the ghost story, tell it in much the same way at the dinner-table'.

Lee also refers to a correspondence in Notes and Queries *for 2 July 1859 which states that*

> *a series of queries on the subject being drawn up at Quebec ... was sent to Colonel Gore of the same garrison, who was understood to be a survivor of the officers who were with Sherbroke and Wynyard at the time of the occurrence, and Colonel Gore explicitly replied to the following effect: He was present at Sydney, in the island of Cape Breton, in the autumn of 1785 or 1786, when the incident happened ... The ghost passed them as they were sitting at coffee, between eight and nine in the evening, and went into G. Wynyard's bed closet, the window of which was pulled down ... I remember the date, and on the 6 June our first letters from England brought the news of John Wynyard's death, [which had happened] on the very night they saw his apparition.*

John Cope Sherbroke and George Wynyard appear in the Army List of 1785, the one as a captain and the other lieutenant in the 33rd Regiment commanded by the Duke of Wellington.

According to a narration resting on the best authority now attainable [John Cope Sherbroke and George Wynyard] were one afternoon sitting in Wynyard's apartment. It was perfectly light, the hour was about four o'clock: they had dined, but neither of them had drunk wine, and they had retired from their mess to continue together the occupations of the morning. It ought to have been said that the apartment in which they were had two doors in it, the one opening into a passage and the other leading into Wynyard's bedroom. There was no other means of entering the sitting-room, so that any person passing into the bedroom must have remained there unless he returned by the way he entered. This point is of consequence to the story.

As these two young officers were pursuing their studies, Sherbroke, whose eyes happened accidentally to glance from the book before him towards the door which opened to the passage, all at once observed a tall youth of about twenty years of age whose appearance was that of extreme emaciation. Struck with the presence of a perfect stranger, he immediately turned to his friend, who was sitting near him, and directed his attention to the guest who had thus strangely broken in upon their studies. As soon as Wynyard's eyes were turned towards the mysterious visitor his countenance became suddenly agitated. 'I have heard,' says Sir John Sherbroke, 'of a man's being as pale as death, but I never saw a living face assume the appearance of a corpse except Wynyard's at that moment.' As they looked silently at the form before them – for Wynyard, who seemed to apprehend the import of the appearance, was deprived of the faculty of speech, and Sherbroke, perceiving the agitation of his friend, felt no inclination to address it – as they looked silently upon the figure it proceeded slowly into the adjoining apartment, and in the act of passing them cast its eyes with an expression of somewhat melancholy affection on young Wynyard. The oppression of this extraordinary presence was no sooner removed than Wynyard, seizing his friend by the arm, and drawing a deep breath as if recovering from the suffocation of intense astonishment and emotion, muttered in a low and almost inaudible tone of voice, 'Great God, my brother!'

'Your brother!' repeated Sherbroke, 'what can you mean? Wynyard, there must be some deception; follow me,' and immediately taking his friend by the arm, he preceded him into the bedroom, which, as before stated, was connected with the sitting-room, and into which the strange visitor had evidently entered ... Imagine the astonishment of the young officers when, on finding themselves in the chamber, they perceived that the room was perfectly untenanted. Wynyard's mind had received an impression at the first moment of his observing him, that the figure whom he had seen was the spirit of his brother. Sherbroke still persevered in strenuously believing that some delusion had been practised. They took note of the day and hour in which the event had happened, but they resolved not to mention the occurrence in the regiment, and gradually they persuaded each other that they had been imposed upon by some artifice of their fellow-officers, though they could neither account for the means of its execution. They were content to imagine anything possible rather than admit the possibility of a supernatural appearance. But though they had attempted these stratagems of self-delusion, Wynyard could not help expressing his solicitude with respect to the safety of the brother whose apparition he had either seen or imagined himself to have seen; and the anxiety which he exhibited for letters from England, and his frequent mention of his brother's health, at length awakened the curiosity of his comrades, and eventually betrayed him into a declaration of the circumstances which he had in vain determined to conceal. The story of the silent and unbidden visitor was no sooner bruited abroad than the arrival of Wynyard's letters from England were welcomed with more than usual eagerness, for they promised to afford the clue to the mystery which had happened among themselves.

By the first ships no intelligence relating to the story could have been received, for they had all departed from England previously to the appearance of the spirit. At length, the long wished-for vessel arrived; all the officers had letters except Wynyard. They examined the several newspapers, but they contained no mention of any death or of any other circumstance connected with his family that could account for the preternatural event. There was a solitary letter for Sherbroke still un-opened. The officers had received their letters in the mess-room at the hour of supper. After Sherbroke had broken the seal of his last packet, and cast a glance on its contents, he beckoned his friend away from the company, and departed from the room. All were silent. The suspense of the interest was now at its climax; the impatience for the return of Sherbroke was inexpressible. They doubted not but that letter had contained the long-expected intelligence.

After the interval of an hour, Sherbroke joined them. No one dared inquire the nature of his correspondence; but they waited in mute attention, expecting that he would himself touch upon the subject. His mind was manifestly full of thoughts that pained, bewildered, and oppressed him. He drew near to the fire-place, and leaning his head on the mantelpiece, after a pause of some moments, said in a low voice to the person who was nearest him, Wynyard's brother was dead. 'Dear John, break to your friend Wynyard the death of his favourite brother.' He had died on the day and at the very hour on which the friends had seen his spirit pass so mysteriously through the apartment.

It might have been imagined that these events would have been sufficient to have impressed the mind of Sherbroke with the conviction of their truth, but so strong was his prepossession against the existence or even the possibility of any preternatural intercourse with the spirits of the departed, that he still entertained a doubt of the report of his senses, supported as their testimony was by the coincidence of sight and event.

Some years after, on his return to England, he was with two gentlemen in Piccadilly, when on the opposite side of the street he saw a person bearing the most striking resemblance to the figure which had been disclosed to Wynyard and himself. His companions were acquainted with the story, and he instantly directed their attention to the gentleman opposite, as the individual who had contrived to enter and depart from Wynyard's apartment without their being conscious of the means. Full of this impression, he immediately went over and addressed the gentleman. He now fully expected to elucidate the mystery. He apologized for the interruption, but excused it by relating the occurrence which had induced him to the commission of this solecism in manners. The gentleman received him as a friend. He had never been out of the country, but he was the twin brother of the youth whose spirit had been seen.

– Lee, *The Other World; Or, Glimpses of the Supernatural*, pp. 26–34.

12. *Talland Bay from the churchyard*
Parson Dodge, the famous ghost-layer, was vicar of Talland in the early eighteenth century. Famed for his ability to subdue devils and ghosts, he was also rumoured to be in league with smugglers on this wild and remote South Cornish coast. See 'Parson Dodge and the Spectral Coach', story no. 33.

13. *The Parish Church of St Peter, Egloshayle, near Wadebridge, Cornwall*
The churchyard, it is said, is haunted by a white rabbit. See 'A Very Dangerous Rabbit', story no. 34.

14. *Portrait of Thomas Hardy, novelist and poet (1840–1928)*
In an interview published in the *Pall Mall Magazine* in 1901, Hardy confessed, 'I am most anxious to believe in what, roughly speaking, we may call the supernatural — but I find no evidence for it!' The story of 'The Dying Mother' (no. 72 in this collection) was narrated during this interview, and another Hardy story, 'Better Company' appears as no. 36. Source of image: The Folklore Society, Ordish Collection.

15. *Notice Board in Boggart Hole Clough, Blackley, Manchester*
Did the legend of the boggart precede the name of this large urban park, or did the name come first? See 'The Boggart of Boggart Hole Clough', story no. 37.

16. *Binham Priory, Norfolk*
Legend has it that a haunted tunnel runs from here to Walsingham. See 'The Fiddler and his Dog', story no. 41.

A seat of the Howard Family

The massive 12th-century earthworks and keep

17. *Detail of a notice board at Castle Rising Castle, Norfolk*
This ancient seat of the Howard family has a haunted tunnel story to rival that told of Binham Priory. Here the tunnel where the fiddler and his dog disappeared is said to run from the castle to Red Mount Chapel in King's Lynn. See 'The Fiddler and his Dog', story no. 41.

Above: 18. *Mannington Hall, near Saxthorpe, Norfolk*
This was the location of one of the best-known personal experience stories of an encounter with a ghost. See 'The Man in the Library', story no. 52.

Left: 19. *The canal bridge near* Woodseaves, *Shropshire*
It was at this place, where Thomas Telford's turnpike road crosses the Birmingham to Liverpool canal, that a Shropshire carrier encountered a terrifying animal ghost. See 'The Man-Monkey', story no. 53.

20. *St Etheldreda's church, Hyssington near Welshpool, Montgomery*
This little church about a mile from the village it serves is, according to legend, the place where a terrible animal ghost was eventually subdued by twelve pious parsons. See 'The Roaring Bull of Bagbury', story no. 60.

21. *Painting of 'The Legend of the Bagbury Bull, Hyssington' in St Etheldreda's church, Hyssington*
See 'The Roaring Bull of Bagbury', story no. 60.

Left: 22. *The 'Scrope' window in St Andrew's church, Bishopsthorpe, North Yorkshire*
The bottom two panels of this 1950s window show Richard le Scrope, Archbishop of York, coming before King Henry IV in May 1405 accused of treason. See 'A Spectral Funeral', story no. 63

Below: 23. *Cattle grazing on the banks of Dozmary Pool, Bodmin Moor, Cornwall*
It was in this desolate spot that the 'Demon Tregeagle' was set to work, emptying the 'bottomless' pool with a holed limpet shell. See 'Tregeagle', story no. 66. Dozmary Pool, a 'Site of Special Scientific Interest', is also popularly famed as the place where King Arthur received the sword Excalibur from the Lady of the Lake.

PART 3

The Nineteenth Century

Introduction

The nineteenth century was the age of the great regional folklore collections, when (to name but a few) men and women such as Robert Hunt (1807–87), Charlotte Burne (1850–1923), Mabel Peacock (1856–1920) and Richard Blakeborough (1850–1924?) were actively searching out specimens of the oral traditions of Great Britain and Ireland. It was the age, too, of theorists such as Andrew Lang (1844–1912) and George Laurence Gomme (1853–1916); and tireless anthologists such as Frederick George Lee (1832–1902), T. F. Thiselton-Dyer (1848–1923) and Sabine Baring-Gould (1834–1924).

It is a truism to say that fashions in ideas, like fashions in design, swing like a pendulum, first dismissing a cultural consensus with disdain, and then enthusiastically reviving it in modified form. However, this does seem to be an accurate picture of what happened in the case of belief in ghosts and apparitions over the course of the nineteenth century. After being initially rejected as absurd, vulgar and unworthy of the interest of serious men and women, ghosts and apparitions became increasingly rehabilitated as objects of study, if not of outright belief, through the operation of cultural forces such the rise of evolutionary theory, the advent of spiritualism, the Romantic movement, the inauguration of the Folklore Society, and a growing interest in all things 'quaint' and 'ancient'.

The themes of nineteenth-century stories do not differ radically from the earlier ones. Revenants still utter prophecies, poltergeists continue to plague unfortunate people and the souls of wicked men and women continue to haunt lonely places, often in animal form, just as they did in the eighteenth century. Ghosts still appear as witnesses to murder, and they still have an interest in buried treasure (though in the nineteenth century rather than guarding it they usually seek to reveal where they have hidden it so that their souls may rest in peace).

Some changes may be detected though. There is a gradual increase in the number of stories about helpful ghosts appearing to strangers to guard them or guide them home (a motif that would become commonplace in the stories of the twentieth century), and there are many comic stories such as 'Short-Hoggers of Whittinghame' (story no. 61) and 'Tommy and the Ghost' (story no. 65). Another difference is that the malign supernatural becomes increasingly distanced from any religious connotations. Even poltergeists become secularised, and 'demons' have been replaced by 'tricksy sprites', 'boggarts' and 'black dogs'.

Whatever the manifestation, however, nineteenth-century people were agog to see whatever there was to see. Mabel Peacock, for example, records that in 1879, 'more than a thousand people' visited the cottage where the Lincolnshire poltergeist was performing, arriving in hordes by train and 'waggonettes' to stand and gape (see story no. 48).

36
Better Company

This story is taken from the memoirs of the Dorset poet and novelist Thomas Hardy (1840–1928).

[The midwife] used to tell a story of a woman who came to consult her about the ghost of another woman she declared she had seen and who 'troubled her' – the deceased wife of the man who was courting her.

'How long hev' the woman been dead?' [the midwife] said.

'Many years!'

'Oh, that were no ghost. Now if she'd only been dead a month or two, and you were making her husband your fancy man, there might have been something in your story. But Lord, much can she care about him after years and years in better company!'

– Hardy, ed. Millgate, *The Life and Works of Thomas Hardy*, p. 316.

37
The Boggart of Boggart Hole Clough

This is probably the most famous of all legends about 'boggarts', defined by Katharine Briggs, the author of The Dictionary of Fairies, *as mischievous brownies (for brownies, see the headnote to 'The Cauld Lad of Hilton', story no. 39). The account below is taken from Charles Hardwick's* Traditions, Superstitions and Folk-Lore of Lancashire*; in turn, Hardwick says he borrowed it from Thomas Crofton Croker (1798–1854) via John Roby's* Traditions of Lancashire *(1829). Readers may be interested to compare it to the Lincolnshire story of the 'Hob Thrust' (story no. 86). Plainly we have here a classic 'migratory legend'.*

In the 1890s Boggart Hole Clough was the location, and cause, of a controversy over free speech. At that time the Clough was an open area of rough grass and sandy slopes forming a natural amphitheatre which, by custom, was often used for political meetings. In 1895 the Corporation of Manchester bought the land and a year later it was decided to ban such gatherings in the Clough. The Pankhursts and Keir Hardy spearheaded a campaign of resistance, Emmeline Pankhurst addressing a meeting of 20,000 in June 1896. After a number of fines, a few imprisonments, and a court case in which Keir Hardy proposed to summon no fewer than 473 witnesses, the case was eventually dropped (see Peters 1984).

Nowadays it is, as Croker describes it, a 'densely wooded dell'. One of Manchester's largest public parks (approximately 67 hectares), it was designated a Local Nature Reserve in November 2007.

Croker makes the scene of his story what was once a retired and densely wooded dell near Manchester, called to this day 'Boggart Ho' Clough'. This boggart sadly pestered a worthy farmer named George Cheetham, by 'scaring his maids, worrying his men, and frightening poor children out of their wits, so that, at last not even a mouse durst show himself indoors at the farm, as he valued his whiskers, after the clock had struck twelve'. This same boggart, however, had some jolly genial qualities. His voice, when he joined the household laughter, on merry tales being told or practical jokes being indulged in, around the hearth at Christmastide, is described as 'small and shrill' and as easily 'heard above the rest, *like a baby's penny trumpet*'. He began to regard himself as a 'privileged inmate' and conducted himself in the most extraordinary manner, snatching the children's bread and butter out of their hands, and interfering with their porridge, milk, and other food. His 'invisible hand' knocked furniture about in the most approved modern style of goblin or spiritual manifestation. Yet this mischievous propensity did not prevent him from occasionally performing some kindly acts, such as churning the cream and scouring the pans and kettles! Truly, he was a 'tricksy sprite' [...]

All this supernatural mountebanking was, it appears, taken in good part by Mr Cheetham's family, and when the children or neighbours wished for a little excitement they easily found it in playing with this eccentric and pugnacious spirit.

But Mr Boggart eventually returned to his old avocations, and midnight noises again disturbed the repose of the inmates of the haunted house. Pewter pots and earthen dishes were dashed to the floor, and yet, in the morning they were found perfectly uninjured, and in their usual places. To such a pitch at last did matters reach, that George Cheetham and his family were observed one day by neighbour John Marshall sullenly following a cart that contained their household goods and chattels. What transpired is best told in Mr Croker's own words:–

'Well, Georgy, and soa you're leaving th'owd house at last,' said Marshall.

'Heigh, Johnny, my lad, I'm in a manner forced to it, thou sees,' replied the other, 'for that wearyfu' boggart torments us soa, we can neither rest neet nor day for't. It seems loike to have a malice again t'young uns, an' it ommost kills my poor dame at thoughts on't, and soa, thou sees, we're forced to flit like.'

He had got thus far in his complaint when behold, a shrill voice, from a deep upright churn, the topmost utensil on the cart, called out, 'Ay, ay, neighbour, we're flitting, you see.'

'Od rot thee,' exclaimed George. 'If I'd known thou'd be flitting too, I wadn't ha' stirred a peg. Nay, nay, it's no use, Mally,' he continued turning to his wife, 'we may as weel turn back again to th'owd house, as to be tormented in another not so convenient.'

– Hardwick, *Traditions, Superstitions and Folk-Lore of Lancashire*, pp. 127–30.

38
The Cauld Lad of Gilsland

The story below, like the following one, comes from William Henderson's Folklore of the Northern Counties *and can be found in his chapter on 'Local Sprites'.*

A friend of mine, born and brought up in the Borders, tells me of [a] Cauld Lad, of whom she heard in her childhood, during a visit to Gilsland, in Cumberland. He perished from cold, at the behest of some cruel uncle or stepdame; and ever after his ghost haunted the family, coming shivering to their bedsides before any one was stricken by illness, his teeth audibly chattering; or, if it were to be fatal, laying his icy hand upon the part which would be the seat of disease, saying,

'Cauld, cauld, aye cauld.
An' ye'se be cauld for evermair.'

– Henderson, *Folklore of the Northern Counties*, p. 230.

39
The Cauld Lad of Hilton

Henderson's second 'Cauld Lad' story comes from Tyne and Wear. Here, he identifies the Cauld Lad as a 'brownie'.

Eminent folklorist the late Katharine Briggs has a very learned entry on brownies in her Dictionary of Fairies *of 1976 (see pp. 45–49). Usually described, she says, as a small man about 3 feet high, raggedly dressed in brown clothes and with a brown face and unkempt hair, a brownie comes out at night and does work that the household servants have left undone. They should be rewarded by laying out a suit of new clothes for them each year. Great care should be taken, however, not to skimp on this gift – clothes of inferior quality will anger the brownie and he will leave the ungrateful household, never to return. The Cauld Lad of Hilton is induced to depart by such a gift however.*

There is the Cauld [cold] Lad of Hilton, who haunted Hilton Castle in the Valley of the Wear. Seldom seen, he was heard night after night by the servants. If they left the kitchen in order, he would amuse himself by hurling everything wildly about; if they left it in confusion, he would arrange everything with the greatest care. Harmless as he seemed, the servants got tired of him; so they laid a green cloak and hood before the kitchen-fire, and set themselves to watch the result. At mid-night the Cauld Lad glided in, surveyed the garments, put them on, frisked about, and when the cock crew, disappeared, saying:

'Here's a cloak, and there's a hood,
The Cauld Lad of Hilton will do no more good.'

All this bespeaks him a sprite of the Brownie type; still he is, in the neighbourhood, deemed the ghost of a servant-boy, slain by an old baron of Hilton, in a moment of passion. The baron, it is said, ordered his horse to be ready at a particular time, waited for it in vain, went to the stable, found the lad asleep, and struck him a blow with a hayfork, which killed him. The baron, it is added, covered the victim with straw till night, and then threw him into a pond, where indeed the skeleton of a boy was discovered years afterwards. Some verses, said to be sung by the Cauld Lad at dead of night, certainly accord well with the notion of his being a ghost:

'Wae's me, wae's me,
The acorn's not yet

Fallen from the tree,
That's to grow the wood;
That's to make the cradle,
That's to rock the bairn,
That's to grow to a man.
That's to lay me!'

– Henderson, *Folklore of the Northern Counties*, p. 230.

40
'Emlyn, Emlyn, Let Me Go'

This story is taken from an article by Justin Simpson in the Stamford Mercury, *Christmas Day, 1891. My thanks to Martin Smith for this item.*

Tradition says that a man named Emlyn, who owned [a small field known as Emlyn's Close in the Northfield area of the town], hanged himself from a tree opposite the Conduit head; and that in consequence it withered and never again bore leaves or showed any sign of life. In my younger days boys used to repeat these words:

'Emlyn, Emlyn, let me go,
Emlyn, Emlyn, bite my toe.'

When thrice incanted after midnight the dead man would appear, seated on a white horse, and gallop round the field. That venerable authority 'the oldest inhabitant' has no recollection of ever seeing the spectre, nor has he heard of anybody who did see it. The legend as to the owner having thrown off this mortal coil in the manner indicated has not a tittle of truth.

– Quoted by Smith, *Stamford Myths and Legends*, p. 70.

41
The Fiddler and His Dog

Legends about lost fiddlers and secret passages are common throughout Britain. Stories very similar to the Norfolk legend below may be found in Cambridgeshire, Durham, Hertfordshire, Shropshire, Gloucestershire, Kent and the Isles of Scilly. What, perhaps, distinguishes the Norfolk stories is that virtually identical versions may be found in locations only a few miles apart, attached to both Binham Priory and Castle Rising Castle.

According to legend, the tiny chapel at Red Mount, St James' Park, Kings Lynn (built 1485) has a secret tunnel linking it to the chapel in Castle Rising. It is said that a drunken fiddler called Curtis decided to explore this tunnel despite its reputation for being haunted. His pet dog went with him and neither fiddler nor dog was ever seen again, though sometimes one can hear the fiddler playing his tunes and the dog whimpering to be let out. The custodian at Castle Rising Castle believes the legend is a folk memory based on the fact that the processional route for pilgrims to the shrine of Our Lady of Walsingham began at Red Mount Chapel and passed through Castle Rising, the pilgrims perhaps making an overnight stop there. The custodian also knew stories of tunnels at Binham, and confirmed that there actually are tunnels there. He said he had explored them himself and could tell us that they were latrine conduits.

Binham Priory, 3–4 miles north-east of Walsingham, is a partly ruined site in the care of English Heritage. Only the nave of the church stands today (the chancel and aisles have gone and, though the very fine arcading below remains intact, the enormous lancet windows in the west end have been bricked in). Nevertheless, what remains is a magnificent example of Norman architecture, grand but full of light. It is still used for services. The Priory's domestic buildings are largely gone now, only broken arches and the shape of old walls showing where they once stood.

It is the story from Binham that is quoted below. It is taken from J. Wentworth Day's 1954 book Here are Ghosts and Witches. *Day says the original story was 'beautifully told in dialect' in* The East Anglian Handbook *in 1892.*

'So you want to go to Binham, eh, sir? Ah, them there old abbeys are funny places and there's funny tales told about 'em. Some on 'em true, tu, as I know well, sir. I s'pose you ha' bin to Walsin'ham?'

I nodded, and the old man went on: 'Walsin'ham was the finest place of the two, I'm told, though Binham had a name er its own. Do you know, sir, there's a subt'tanim passage atween them two, right underground. You can see it as you goo along the road, runnin' across the medders like a grate green bank and I ha' sin 'em a-borin' down to try an' find out mor about it – specially where it cross the road and where you can hear the holler sound on't as you drive over it. Them old monks used to be up to curis [curious] kind o' games, and I 'spect that when they got kinder tired o' their own company they used to goo tru this underground passage to see the folks at the other end. Went a-wisitin' yer know, sir.

'Thare are folks who say that once was the time that every night a grate tall feller, like an old monk, and dressed in black, used to walk along on top o' the bank right from Walsin'ham to Binham, shakin' his ugly owd hid and 'pearin' just as if he was a-lookin' fer suffin' he could never find. I ha' never sin him, but my grandsir hev many a time, though none ever clapped eyes on him sin the fiddler went down thare and never cum back.

'Yer see, sir, once was the time that sum of the bank, close to the abbey, kinder caved in, and a lot on 'em went to see it and to peep into the dark old passage. They daren't goo in, or at least, not for far, but while they were a-poakin' and a-paarin' who should come up but old Jimmy Griggs the fiddler. Jimmy was afeared o' naught and he sa'; "Clear away, together, I'm a-goin' in," and in he went and his dog Trap with him.

'Jimmy had his fiddle with him, and he sa'; "I'll keep on a-playin' and yow together goo along the top o' the bank and then yow'll know whare I am." An', so they did an' they haard him a-playin' under the ground, just one tune and then another. All er a sudden the tune stopped and they couldn't hear anything. They called and shouted but, sir, my grandsir said as how there wor never a sound.

'Sum said one thing and sum said another, but while they were a-considerin' what tu du, one on 'em sa'; "Why if here ain't old Trap" and thare was the dog beside 'em sure enuff, with his tail atween his legs and a-shiverin' as if he wor mortal skeered.

'They went back to the hole, sir, and peeped in but it wor dark as the grave and jest as quiet. They never saw Jimmy any more, and in the night thare was a storm such as they had never known afore, and when mornin' came that place whare he went in was all broken down 'er haap and folks told the tale far and wide that Jimmy Griggs the fiddler had been carried off by the Black Monk.

'Yes, sir, I s'pose they ought to ha' sarched further, but they didn't and poor old Griggs had ne'er a friend to trouble arter him and we haard no more about it. But ever sin' then they ha' called that bank "Fiddler's Hill".'

– *The East Anglian Handbook, Yearbook and Scrapbook*, Norwich 1892. Quoted by Day, *Here are Ghosts and Witches*, pp. 138–40.

42
'For Ever and Ay; For a Year and a Day'

Richard Blakeborough, whose lively account I quote below, being interested in folk speech, renders the dialogue between the exorcist and the ghost in this story in dialect. For the sake of readability I have regularised the English.

Carthorpe and Burneston, mentioned in the story, are both near Bedale, North Yorkshire.

Compare the brevity of the exorcism in this story to the lengthy and complex procedures told of in 'The Great Giant of Henllys' and 'The Roaring Bull of Bagbury' (stories no. 26 and 60 respectively).

A certain house in Carthorpe was suspected of being witch-held, and everything about the place witch-stricken, and for some time neither land nor beast throve. It happened that a man who had the power of smelling witches slept for a night under this particular roof. In the morning he said that they were quite mistaken in supposing the house witch-held, declaring that it was haunted. He advised them to prevail upon the parson to shout it down.

The Rector of Burneston, having been seen, kindly undertook the shouting down. To this end he partook of a good meal, and then betook himself to the farmer's well. There he read something out of the Prayer Book, which brought the spirit up to the well's head, and then the parson called out: 'For ever and for ay' to which the spirit replied, 'For a year and a day.' Then the parson kept at it, and the spirit did the same, and they both went at it like that for over two hours, but the parson got the last word because the spirit couldn't hold out any longer, and so the parson won the battle in the end, and conjured it down; and so that spirit never again, at any time ever again, could come out of the bad place to work ill against anybody.

– Blakeborough, *Wit, Character, Folklore and Customs of the North Riding of Yorkshire*, pp. 160–61.

43
The Ghost in the Cupboard

The writer quoted here (Mary Lewes), introduces the tale with this preamble: 'Mayfield [is] a very old house in West Wales, dating back to the year 1600. Among the family portraits there, one is shown the picture of a young lady in the dress of the eighteenth century. This was a Mrs Jones (Jones shall replace the real name of the family) and an ancestress of the present owner of the house. Tradition says that a wicked butler murdered this poor lady in a large cupboard "almost a little room" which opens out of the dining-room. He then fled with the family plate, but finding it too heavy, he dropped part of his plunder in a ditch near the house, where it was subsequently found. Ever since then, the ghost of the murdered lady walks out of the cupboard every Christmas evening (the anniversary of the tragedy), never appearing till the ladies have left the dinner-table. At least, so runs the tale; and now for the sequel.'

Early in the last century, Mayfield and the property were owned by a certain Jones, who had a brother living in India. Whether Mr Jones was a bachelor or widower at the time of the following occurrence, one does not know, but at all events he lived at Mayfield by himself. He used the dining-room as a sitting-room of an evening, and after his dinner would turn his chair round to the fire, and sit there reading till it was bed-time. One night he had sat up later than usual, and as he shut up his book and bethought him of bed, the clock struck midnight. In the corner of the room, behind his chair, was the cupboard already referred to. Now as the last stroke of twelve died away, Mr Jones heard the click of the door opening. He turned his head and there, walking out of the cupboard towards him, he saw the figure of a woman dressed in an old-fashioned costume. She advanced a few paces, stopped, and said in loud, clear tones, 'Your brother is dead.' Then she turned and walked back into the cupboard, the door of which shut with a loud clang. As soon as he recovered from his astonishment, Mr Jones made a thorough search of the cupboard and room, but could find no trace of any inmate. Convinced at length that a message from the other world had been brought to him, he made a careful note of the date and hour of the incident.

In those days letters took a long while to travel from India to this country, and he had therefore many weeks to wait before the mail brought him news that his brother had died, the time of death coinciding exactly with the night and hour in which he was warned by the apparition at Mayfield.

– Lewes, *Stranger Than Fiction*, pp. 32–33.

44
The Golden King of Bryn-yr-Ellylon

In October 1833 a farmer near Mold in Flintshire, wishing to level a field, uncovered a Bronze Age tumulus containing fragments of what was identified as a breastplate or corselet dating from 1900 to 1600 BC. With the corselet there were some amber beads, a skull and a considerable number of small bones, none of them longer than 2–3 inches. The fragments of the corselet were shared out between the landowner and his workmen but were eventually reunited and reassembled at the British Museum, where it is now on display.

Stories about a 'golden knight' quickly proliferated, many sightings claiming to pre-date the finding of the Bronze Age hoard, and the story began to acquire typical 'ghost legend' motifs – the small bones became a 'skeleton', mysterious music had been heard, locals had long known the site was haunted, and an old woman returning from market (or, in one account, fetching her husband back from the pub), was said to have seen a man of unusual size, clothed in a coat of gold which shone like the sun. Commentators were soon speculating that memories of the burial had remained in the area for 1,400 years, though turned now into a ghost story.

The earliest accounts of the legend are more or less contemporaneous with the discovery of the corselet. These are:

A review of Tales about Wales, with a Catechism of Welsh History by a Lady of the Principality *(Mrs Eliza Constantia Campbell), which was published in the September–December number of* The Monthly Review, or, Literary Journal *of 1837 (this quotes a letter sent to Mrs Campbell in 1834).*

An article entitled 'A letter from John Gage, esq FRS, Director, to Sir Henry Bell KH FRS, Secretary, accompanying a Gold British Corselet exhibited to the Society, and since purchased by the Trustees of the British Museum', published as article XXII in Archaeologia: or Miscellaneous Tracts Relating to Antiquity, *vol. 26, 1835 (this includes an extract of a letter from the Revd Clough, Vicar of Mold).*

The poem printed below, which was written in 1861 by the vicar's wife.

An account from Chambers' Book of Days, *published in 1869.*

Later redactions may be found on the internet and in Peter Underwood's Ghosts of Wales *and Richard Holland's* Supernatural Clwyd.

It is interesting to note that the artefact is now thought to more probably have been a cape worn by a high-ranking woman (see http://news.bbc.co.uk/1/hi/wales/north_east/4283562.stm). A housing estate now covers the former site of Bryn-yr-Ellylon.

The Field of the Golden Corselet

There is a vale, in Cambria's northern shire,
Fertile and gay, girdled with sunny hills.
Little increase of beauty need desire
The gazer, save enlargement of the rills
Which sparkle in its bosom; clear and bright
And rapid are they, but the summer light
Scarce meets reflection there; unless the trees
So thickly clustered, feel the stirring breeze.

[...]

A road winds gently up a steep incline,
Sheltering with hedges high its wavering line;
On one side fields of corn, and here and there
A dusky coal shaft, with its margin bare.
A hay field on the other side you see,
With no especial mark of mystery.
Yet was this ever called the Field of Gold,
And yon the Fairy Hill, since times of old.
For there where lines of gravel mark the green,
A wavering light at eventide was seen,
And when the first faint stars came peeping through
A dewy moonlit sky of palest blue,
A mist-robed form stood with imperial mien
Or sadly bent him o'er the flowery green.
None saw the face but faint and shining there,
The snowy garments fluttered in the air.
Veiled was the head, as ancient Druids wore
Their priestly robes, and the long right arm bore
What might be sword or sceptre – many stayed
At the low gate an instant, then dismayed
Muttering a prayer ran homewards; none dared face
The awful unknown in his dwelling place.
And sometimes low sweet music stole around
And drew all ears to listen to the sound.
With a faint passionate cadence of lament,
Such as once thrilled from a dead warrior's tent
When o'er the senseless form his deeds were sung
Ere in the grave they laid him; while each tongue
Hymned his departed glory. – Then there rang
A fuller tone as of a trumpet's clang.
And then the fairy music died away,
And left the moonbeams on the hill to play
Lonely and silent; and the aged men
Who dwelt in yonder hamlet in the glen,
Would warn the children – 'Go ye not too near,'
'The Ancient King walks there, behold, and fear.'

Such in my days of childhood, was the tale
That thrilled my fancy in the lovely vale.
Nor was inquiry made by anyone,
How rose the tale, though well and widely known.
But once it happened, men were set to seek
For gravel 'neath the greensward; week by week
They laboured, till they came to heavy stones,
Which broken – there lay dust of human bones!
This, with rude earthenware and pottery slight
Away they throw, till carelessly they light
On something large and bright – 'What may this be?'
E'en the rude workmen mutter, as they see
The thin bright metal shine. 'There, put it down,'
'We'll take it to the master in the town,
'He'll maybe give us somewhat for the thing
'Will help to pay our weekly reckoning.
'For these great stones have wasted so our time
'We ne'er shall make our wages!' – Oh that rhyme
Must chronicle such deeds! The rescued 'thing'
Was the Gold Corslet of the ancient King!
The stone his coffin, and that scattered dust
All that remained of the brave and just!

[...]

The gravel pit is closed, once more there
The harebell quivers in the evening air.
But the dread form has vanished, never more
Over his desecrated grave to soar.
Nor ring the Fairy harps their requiem low,
Now the old Hero sleeps no more below.
His name is doubtful; though old legends tell
Of Benlli Gawr, who wisely ruled and well.
Who gave his name to yonder mountain high,
A name oft Heard in ancient battle cry,
And who in Bardic songs is ever hight,
'Benlli of golden Torques, pure and bright!'

– M. B. C. *Scenes and Stories Little Known, Chiefly in North Wales*, n.p.

45
Humphrey's Hitch-Hiker

This story can also be found in Katharine Briggs's mammoth dictionary of folktales and legends under the title 'The Pillion Lady' (See Briggs, A Dictionary of British Folk-Tales in the English Language, part B, Folk Legends, *vol. 1, p. 556). Her source is Bowker's* Goblin Tales of Lancashire, *as cited below.*

There are two bridges over the River Wyre at Garstang, the most southerly being the more probable scene of Humphrey's adventure. Now popular with dog-walkers, a lane runs down to an aqueduct, a ford and a bridge, then turning sharp right then left, leads directly to a number of farmsteads.

One night in summer, Humphrey Dobson, having spent a day at Garstang Market, and followed it with a jovial evening in the Frances Arms, mounted his mare to return home. On the way they came to a place where the road crossed a stream, and this spot was said to be haunted by a woman who had been murdered there many years before. Humphrey attempted to disregard this tale, and sang bravely as he approached the bridge. But as soon as the mare set foot upon it, Humphrey heard an unearthly laugh from under the arch, and suddenly an ice-cold arm came round his waist, and he knew that something was riding behind him.

The mare flew as she had never flown before, and soon they reached the farmhouse. But his efforts to guide her into the yard were useless, and she sped on past the gate. Humphrey heard another laugh, this time close behind him; and, turning for the first time, he saw riding at his back a skull, with eyeless sockets, and gleaming teeth, and felt the pressure of the arm tighten around him.

He put down his hand to loosen it, and found that it was that of a skeleton.

They rode on and on, till at last the mare stumbled, and Humphrey was thrown violently off. He was stunned, and did not regain consciousness till the sun was high. He struggled home, faint with loss of blood and the pain of his injuries, leading the old mare, who was unhurt. Many in the village professed to disbelieve his story, but it was long before any would venture to cross the old bridge after dark.

– Bowker, *Goblin Tales of Lancashire*, p. 77.

46
The Lady of Littledean

At the beginning of the chapter in which this story appears, the author, William Henderson, says: 'The universal voice of mankind has ever pointed out certain places as the borderland between the material and the spiritual world – has, truly or falsely, indicated deserted houses, marshy wastes, lonely roads, spots where enormous crimes have been perpetrated, and so forth, as haunted. In general, places which once were closely connected with man, but are now deserted by him, are thus distinguished in the popular mind, rather than those which have always been barren and desolate. It is natural, then, that with a past rich in historic incidents of the wildest kind, we have many haunted spots in the North.'

Littledean Tower, the remains of a four-storey sixteenth-century tower house in the care of the Royal Commission on the Ancient and Historic Monuments of Scotland, is near Maxton, Roxburghshire and occupies the site of an earlier (possibly pre-historic) fort.

The old tower of Littledean, on the Tweed side, had long been haunted by the spirit of an old lady, once its mistress, who had been a covetous, grasping woman, and oppressive to the poor. Tradition averred that she had amassed a large sum of money by thrift or extortion, and now could not rest in her grave because of it. Spite of its ghost, however, Littledean Tower was inhabited by a laird and his family, who found no fault with their place of abode, and were not much troubled by thoughts of the supernatural world. One Saturday evening, however, a servant-girl, who was cleaning shoes in the kitchen by herself, suddenly observed an elf-light shining on the floor. While she gazed on it, it disappeared, and in its place stood an old woman wrapped in a brown cloak, who muttered something about being cold, and asked to warm herself at the fire. The girl readily consented, and seeing that her visitor's shoes were wet, and her toes peeping out blue and cold from their tips, she good-naturedly offered to dry and clean the shoes, and did so. The old lady, touched by this attention, confessed herself frankly to be the apparition that haunted the house. 'My gold wud na let me rest,' said she, 'but I'll tell ye where it lies; 'tis 'neath the lowest step o' the Tower stairs. Take the laird there, an' tell him what I now tell ye; then dig up the treasure, and put it in his hands. An' tell him to part it in two shares: one share let him keep, for he's master here now; the other share he maun part again, and gie half to you, for ye are a kind lassie and a true, and half he maun gie to the poor o' Maxton, the auld folk and the fatherless bairns, and them that need it most. Do this an' I shall rest in my grave, where I've no rested yet, and never will I trouble the house mair till the day o' doom.' The girl rubbed her eyes, looked again, and behold the old woman was gone!

Next morning the young servant took her master to the spot which had been indicated to her, and told him what had taken place. The stone was removed, and the treasure discovered, and divided according to the instructions given. The laird, being blessed with a goodly family of sturdy lads and smiling maidens, found no difficulty in disposing of his share. The servant-girl, so richly dowered, found a good husband ere the year had passed. The poor of Maxton, for the first time in their lives, blessed the old lady of Littledean; and never was the ancient tower troubled again by ghost or apparition.

– Henderson, *Folklore of the Northern Counties*, p. 271.

47
The Laying of Benjie Gear

T. F. Thiselton-Dyer, whose account is reproduced here, ascribes the story to 'Mr James Spry', writing in The Western Antiquary. *He does not give a date. Cranmere Pool is a small depression in the peat on Dartmoor which nowadays only has water in it after heavy rains. The pool has interest apart from being the place where the ghost of Benjie Gear was laid: it is the location of the first ever post-box, erected in 1854 for walkers to leave notes of their routes etc. Cranmere pool is now within the boundaries of Okehampton artillery range, and may only be approached at certain dates and times.*

'Now thou art come, I must be gone,' the phrase the vanquished spectre ejaculates when faced with the Arabic-speaking clergyman, is a common motif in Cornish ghost legends. It is, for example, virtually identical with that used by the driver of the spectral coach in the story of 'Parson Dodge and the Spectral Coach' (no. 33).

A ghost known as 'Benjie Gear' long troubled the good people of Okehampton to such an extent that at last the aid of the archdeacon was called in, and the clergy were assembled in order that the troubled spirit might be laid and cease to trouble them. There were twenty-three of the clergy who invoked him in various classic languages, but the insubordinate spirit refused to listen to their request. At length, one more learned than the rest addressed him in Arabic, to which he was forced to succumb, saying, 'Now thou art come, I must be gone!' He was then compelled to take the form of a colt; a new bridle and bit, which had never been used, were produced, with a rider, to whom the Sacrament was administered. The man was directed to ride the colt to Cranmere Pool, on

Dartmoor, the following instructions being given him. He was to prevent the colt from turning its head towards the town until they were out of the park, and then make straight for the pool, and when he got to the slope, to slip from the colt's back, pull the bridle off, and let him go. All this was dexterously performed, and the impetus thus gained by the animal with the intention of throwing the rider over its head into the Pool, accomplished its own fate.

– Thiselton-Dyer, *The Ghost World*, pp. 195–96.

48
A Lincolnshire Poltergeist

Mabel Peacock, the Lincolnshire folklorist who collected this account, included it in her chapter on witchcraft, and it would appear that most of the local people who witnessed these events or heard about them would have agreed with her. Today, of course, most people would see this as a classic poltergeist story.

On Sunday 23 February 1879, great excitement was caused by an out-break of witchcraft in a village between the Ancholme and the Trent. From the floor of the lower room of a cottage bricks began to leap from their places onto the sofa, into the fire, or through the window. The crockery and tin cans moved from their shelves, an earthen 'pancheon' full of flour flew three times round the house – that is the ordinary dwelling-room, where the cooking is done – it then flung its contents on the doorstep, while a saucepan passed through the window empty, and returned full of water which it poured over the floor. All this is what report said. The old man who was the tenant of the house asserted that the spirits first began to 'play up' on Friday when the pig escaped from its sty by unknown means. The bricks of the floor became lively on Saturday, then one of them dashed with such violence against the ceiling that it made a dint on the wood. Also, several plates had walked upstairs, and the kettle had flown off the fire and scalded him so severely he began to think 'it was time to flit'.

The landlord of the house concluded from these manifestations that the devil was in the place. He therefore announced that he should keep watch through the following night with a chosen band of religious associates, and take refuge in prayer if the fiend came to question him. Several other people gathered round the building to see signs and wonders, agreed with him that Satan was the cause of the mischief, and were understood to remark that those who doubted the power of the Evil One in this world, would have ample reason for certitude in the next. The general opinion, however, seemed to be that the infernal powers had only an indirect connection with the disturbance, and that some witch was the immediate cause of the 'do'. One sight-seer suggested that possibly a ghost might have caused the racket, in which case it must be the spirit of someone who had been buried during the last twenty-five years, because it is a known fact that the dead are bound to begin action within that time if they are going to walk.

When the local policeman reached the cottage the tenant seemed scarcely willing to speak of his remarkable experiences, and informed that official that it was his grand-daughter of fourteen who had 'seen the best part of the spirit work'. But another witness came forward to state that on Friday night he sat up armed with a knife, and himself saw a brick fly up from the ground. He thought that a 'moudiwarp' [mole] might be at work under the floor, so he prodded about with his weapon but discovered nothing.

After the policeman's departure the tenant became more communicative. He now recollected seeing a basket of wurzels which had been placed on a brick to prevent it rising from its place, dash itself against the ceiling. A can of water had also walked upstairs 'step by step'. At nine o'clock in the evening the cottage was full of people. Among the rest was the landlord who dolorously remarked that he could not expect his tenant to pay for the broken windowpanes, if spirits, as seemed likely, were to blame for the destruction.

Another man observed that he was convinced that the blood of the witch who had done the damage must be drawn before this game would stop; and a third speaker expressed the opinion that the tenant's grand-daughter was the agent, causing the trouble under the influence of an evil power which she was bound to obey.

During the night the house was quiet, but early on Monday a pot of lard cast itself down the staircase from an upper room in which the grand-daughter happened to be alone. At a later time a box of paper also fell from the same room. When questioned, the girl said that she had had naught to do with the matter, and pointed to the place where the box had been standing before it bestirred itself. According to an unbeliever who happened to be in the house, a line of footprints ran towards this spot, and he held they had been formed by ordinary human agency. After these events the girl was sent into another bed-room, into which she appeared very unwilling to go, professing that she was scared. However, under pressure, she went and was heard to cross the chamber with deliberate heavy steps, and pause by the window. Then, according to the unbeliever, there followed sounds as of stealthy movements. These were scarcely audible through the floor, still they were to be detected, and soon a green cushion fell down the stairs. The landlord, when he heard of these later occurrences observed that he 'never rightly believed as it was spirits,' but he would not deny that the girl might be possessed, and unable to keep herself from mischief. Meanwhile, a company of New Revivalists, hearing various accounts of what was happening from people in whom imagination was more highly developed than was historical accuracy, concluded that whatever the power at work might be, they ought to pray it out of the neighbourhood. With this object in view they arrived to hold an assembly in the cottage, and as a beginning removed from the floor a number of the remaining bricks in order to search for the cause of the trouble.

On Monday afternoon the police sergeant again came, but after consulting with a magistrate he concluded that modern English law provides no remedy for witch-work. No active steps could be taken unless the tenant would consent to assume that an earthly being using ordinary means, was responsible for the injury done.

The girl who was suspected of being the medium through whom the marvels were worked was urged to acknowledge her part in the matter, but she listened to what was said with stony indifference, merely denying that she had any connection with the dancing bricks and dishes. Every question was met by the assertion that she knew nothing about it, but that she was frightened. Finally she was sent away for a time, to give the witch, ghost, or devil, an opportunity of continuing the commotion in her absence, if able to do so.

After the girl had gone the unseen powers lost their interest in the place. The usual quiet was restored, though for some days strangers, lured by the wildest tales, came from a distance by train, and by waggonette to gaze on the spot. It was calculated that more than a thousand people visited the cottage. One of them was a woman known to be a witch by descent. This good dame was an object of somewhat painful interest to several of the crowd, who were observed to protect themselves from her glance by doubling a fist with the tip of the thumb protruding between the index and the middle fingers, after the fashion of those who desire to avert the evil eye.

At a later date, it was said that a woman relation of the grand-daughter (known as the witchcraft girl) hung wicken [rowan] tree over the hearth to put an end to her peculiar power, but she was a witch of such a confirmed type that even wicken was of no use.

In the summer of 1889 her witchcraft broke out again. A letter written on the subject on July 22nd of that year related that she 'has been lodging with some respectable people and has been on the parish and ill for some weeks. A day or two ago manifestations began. The most noteworthy seems to have been that the salt emptied itself into the sugar without the aid of human hands. She seems to have held a levee on Saturday. She sent for two men whose sons were ill, and assured them that she had not caused it, but that she had been the cause of the manifestations at —'.

In a later letter: 'I think I told you that the witchcraft girl had been sent to the Union [workhouse], and thence to the Lincoln Asylum. M. met a man yesterday who said that the person she lodged with had said to her after the first time the salt emptied itself into the sugar, "Noo then, my lass, you can't make it do that agean wi'oot tuchin' it."

"Git sum moore salt," she replied, "an' you'll soon see."

More salt was got, and as a matter of course it progressed by itself and turned over into the sugar-basin. The same man also related that when they got her to the Brigg Union they put her in the washing-place. As soon as she entered all the water ran out of the tubs, just as if there were large bung-holes in their bottoms. As soon as she was sent out of the room the water remained in the tubs as usual, but no sooner did she re-enter than the same phenomena manifested themselves.

After some time in the Lincoln Asylum the girl seemed better and was discharged. She died young however. People who had no belief in witchcraft thought that she began to suffer from a severe and mischievous form of hysteria when she was about fourteen. Those who knew her well said that she was often 'queer' and suffered from ill health.

Mrs I. once told [Wilhelmine Fowler] that she herself had 'lodged for a time with the witchcraft girl.' While she was there the witch was ill with typhoid fever, and Mrs I. helped to nurse her. One night, during the illness she was suddenly seized with what the women present took for a fit. She became quite stiff, and her body was so hard and 'trig' [tight, firm] it was impossible to make any impression upon it. She was lying right at the edge of a big double bed. Mrs I. was standing at the foot watching her when suddenly she began to laugh, and still keeping the rest of her body quite stiff, passed the arm next to the edge of the bed under her head. The arm at once 'grew out ever so much too long', so that she was able to reach the pillow on the far side of the bed. She threw this at the watchers and at once became rigid again. This she did twice, to the great astonishment of all present. Mrs I. also related that when the girl went to K— she used to frighten people so much no one would go near the house she was in. 'Every night the tall old-fashioned clocks used to walk about the house striking twenty-four, and pitchers full of cream came out of the dairy. Once all the china began "chittering" about on the cupboard shelves.'

– Bennett, ed., *Mabel Peacock's Folklore and Legends of Lincolnshire*, CD ROM, Chapter 4.

49
The Lledrith

As an introduction to this story, T. F. Thiselton-Dyer writes, 'The Scotch wraith and Irish fetch have their parallel in Wales in the Lledrith, or spectre of a person seen before his death. It never speaks, and vanishes if spoken to. It has been seen by miners previous to a fatal accident in the mine.'

The story is told of a miner who saw himself lying dead and horribly maimed in a phantom tram-car, led by a phantom horse, and surrounded by phantom miners. As he watched this dreadful group of spectres they passed on, looking neither to the right nor the left, and faded away. The miner's dog was as frightened as its master, and ran away howling. The miner continued to work in the pit, and as the days passed on and no harm came to him he grew more cheerful, and was so bold as to laugh at the superstition. But the day he did this a stone fell from the roof and broke his arm. As soon as he recovered he resumed work in the pit; but a stone crushed him, and he was borne maimed and dead in the tram along the road where his 'lledrith' had appeared.

– Thiselton-Dyer, *The Ghost World*, pp. 370–71.

50
The Lovers of Porthangwartha

This romantic story relies on continuing beliefs about the ability of dying people to appear to those they love, and also the notion that the dead may return to accompany those they loved to the other world when they, too, are ready to die.

The name 'Porthangwartha' does not appear on maps of Cornwall, but 'Porthgwarra', renowned as a bird-watchers' paradise 2 miles from Land's End, claims the legend for its own. The Cornish Tourist Board website tells the story of 'Sweethearts' Cove' at Porthgwarra. The entry reads, 'The story goes that two young lovers, Nancy and William, who were forbidden to meet arranged an assignation here before William went to sea. Months passed and he did not return home and Nancy was beside herself with worry. One evening she went to the beach and stood in the sea on an incoming tide. As the sea washed around her a sailor was seen to appear and put his arms around her whereupon both Nancy and the sailor disappeared. News soon arrived in Porthgwarra that William's ship had been wrecked with the loss of all its crew. The couple had found each other finally in death.' (See http://www.intocornwall.com/engine/azabout.asp?guide=Porthgwarra).

Hunt's version is decidedly more poetic, but the ending is ambiguous. It is not clear whether the girl was still alive or already dead when spotted at the cove; either interpretation fits both the plot and the tradition.

The names of the youth and maiden who fixed the term 'Lovers' Cove' upon this retired spot have passed from the memory of man. A simple story, however, remains ...

The course of love with this humble pair did not run smooth. On one side or the other the parents were decidedly opposed to the intimacy which existed, and by their persecutions, they so far succeeded, that the young man was compelled to immigrate to some far distant land.

In this cove the lovers met for the last time in life, and vowed under the light of the full moon, that living or dead they would meet at the end of three years.

The young woman remained with her friends – the young man went to the Indies. Time passed on, and the three years, which had been melancholy to both, were expiring.

One moonlight night, when the sea was tranquil as a mirror, an old crone sat on the edge of the cliff 'making her charms'. She saw a figure – she was sure it was a spirit, very like the village maiden – descend into the cove, and seat herself upon a rock, around two-thirds of which the light waves were rippling. On this rock sat the maiden, looking anxiously out over the sea, until, from the rising of the tide, she was completely surrounded. The old woman called; but in vain – the maiden was unconscious of any voice. There she sat, and the tide was rising rapidly round her. The old woman, now seeing the danger in which she was, resolved to go down into the cove, and, if possible, to awaken the maiden to a sense of her danger. To do this, it was necessary to go round a projecting pile of rocks. While doing this, she lost sight of the object of her interest, and much was her surprise, when she again saw the maiden, to perceive a young sailor by her side, his arm around her waist. Conceiving that help had arrived, the old woman sat herself down on the slope of the descending path, and resolved patiently to await the arrival of the pair on shore, and then to [be]rate the girl soundly.

She sat watching this loving and lovely pair, lighted as they were on the black rock by a full flood of moonshine. There they sat, and the tide rose and washed round them. Never were boy and girl so mad, and at last the terrified old woman shrieked with excitement. Suddenly they appeared to float off upon the waters. She thought she heard their voices; but there was no sound of terror. Instead of it a tranquil murmuring music, like the voice of doves, singing,

I am thine
Thou art mine
Beyond control;
In the wave
In the grave
Of heart and soul.

Down, down into the sea passed the lovers. Awestruck, the old woman looked on, until, as she said, 'At last they turned round, looked me full in the face, smiling like angels, and, kissing each other, sank to rise no more.'

They tell us that the body of the young woman was found a day or two after in a neighbouring cove, and that intelligence eventually reached England that the young man had been killed on this very night.

– Hunt, *Popular Romances of the West of England*, pp. 247–48.

51
Madam Pigott

According to the folklorist Charlotte Burne, who recorded this Shropshire story in the mid-nineteenth century, 'This wild and gruesome myth is familiar to the poor folk for miles around.'

When we visited Chetwynd Park in December 2011 to take photographs, we could find no sign of 'Madam Pigott's chair', but a dog-walker we spoke to knew the story of Madam Pigott and said that, as a boy, he had believed the road to be haunted. Chetwynd Hall was pulled down in 1964.

Madam Pigott [is] the ancient terror of Chetwynd and Edgmond. Village tradition (utterly unsupported by genealogical evidence) declares that long ago, no one can tell when, some one or other of the many Madam Pigotts who have in turn reigned in the old family mansion at Chetwynd, was an unloved and neglected wife. When her baby was born, so the story goes, her husband showed no anxiety for her safety, provided his child lived, and on being told of her extreme danger only replied that 'one should lop the root to save the branch'. Neither mother nor child survived, but after her husband had thus cruelly willed her death, Madam Pigott's spirit could find no rest. Night after night, exactly at twelve o'clock, she issued from a trap-door in the roof of Chetwynd (old) Rectory, and wandered through the park and the lanes in the direction of Edgmond, turning over, as she passed it, a large boulder-stone by the roadside between Edgmond and Newport. Her favourite haunt was the steep, dark, high-banked lane, properly called Cheney Hill, but nearly as well known by the name of Madam Pigott's Hill. Near the top of it was a curiously-twisted tree-root called 'Madam Pigott's Armchair'. On this, or else on the stone wall of Chetwynd Park just above it, Madam Pigott used to sit, 'on a moonshiny night', combing her baby's hair; and if some rider passed by (especially if he were on any errand concerning a woman in the same circumstances as herself), she and her black cat would spring up behind him and cling fast, notwithstanding all his efforts, till she came to a 'running water', then she could go no farther.

At last she became so troublesome that twelve of the neighbouring clergy were summoned to lay her, by incessantly reading psalms till they made her obedient to their power. Mr Foy, curate of Edgmond, has the credit of having been the one to succeed in this, for he continued to 'read' after all the others were exhausted. Yet at least ten or twelve years after his death, some fresh alarm of Madam Pigott arose, and a party went in haste to beg a neighbouring rector to come and lay the ghost! And to this day, Chetwynd Hall – which some say was the starting-point of the ghostly ramble – has the reputation of being haunted, and many a strong young groom or ploughboy still shrinks from facing 'Madam Pigott's Hill' after dark.

One old dame, coeval with the century, and now (1883) living in Castle Street, Eccleshall, claims to have actually seen Madam Pigott herself, in her childhood. According to her, the unhappy lady was the wife of the last of the Chetwynd Pigotts, who, after her death, was so troubled by her spirit that he shut up his house and went abroad, and eventually sold the property rather than live there. (It is needless to say that the estate was sold, about 1780, for quite other reasons.) The uncle and aunt of Mrs Garratt – so our old friend is called – were put in charge of the house at a time when it stood empty, early in the present century, and she stayed with them there when a very little girl. Often, she now declares, when she looked out of the window on a moonlight night, she saw a pale white figure sadly and silently wandering about the garden. Strange noises, too, were heard within the house, and when the little girl was frightened by these mysterious sounds, her aunt would say, 'Never mind, child, it's only Madam Pigott coming. Put your apron over your head when she goes by, and she'll do you no harm.'

– Burne, *Shropshire Folklore*, pp. 124–27.

52
The Man in the Library

In his introduction to his collection of essays, Frivola, *published in 1896, the scholar, cleric and writer Augustus Jessopp (1823–1914) explains that this essay appeared first in the* Athenaeum *of 10 January 1880, and had produced 'such an immense sensation at the time' that he had since been 'compelled to relate the facts by word of mouth' again and again. Consequently he 'thought it better to re-issue the narrative ... and save [himself] from having to repeat the old story'.*

Mannington Hall, an archetypal 'moated grange', is near Saxthorpe, Norfolk. It has been in the Walpole family since 1736.

On the tenth of October, 1879, I drove over from Norwich to Mannington Hall, to spend the night at Lord Orford's. Though I was in perfect health and high spirits, it is fair to state that for some weeks previously I had had a great deal to think about, some little anxiety, and considerable mental strain of one kind or another. I was not, however, conscious of anything approaching weariness, irritability or 'fag'. I arrived at 4 p.m. and was engaged in pleasant and animated conversation until it was time to dress for dinner. We dined at seven; our party numbered six persons. Of these, four at least had been great travellers. I myself was rather a listener; the talk was general and discursive, and amused and interested me greatly. Not for a single moment did it turn upon the supernatural; it was chiefly concerned with questions of art and the experiences of those who had seen a great deal of the world and could describe intelligently what they had seen and comment upon it suggestively. I have rarely been at a more pleasant party. After dinner we played a rubber [of whist]. We left off as we began, and as two of the guests had some distance to drive, we broke up at half past ten.

The main object of my going over to Mannington was to examine and take notes upon some very rare books in Lord Orford's library, which I had been anxiously wishing to get a sight of for some years, but had never been so fortunate enough to meet with up to this time. I asked leave to sit up for some hours and make transcripts. His lordship at first wished me to let his valet remain in attendance to see that all lights were put out, but as this would have embarrassed me and compelled me to go to bed earlier than I wished, and as it seemed likely that I should be occupied till two or three o'clock in the morning, it was agreed that I should be left to my own devices and that the servant should be allowed to retire. By eleven o'clock, I was the only person downstairs, and I was very soon busily at work and absorbed in my occupation.

The room in which I was writing is a large one, with a huge fireplace and a grand old chimney; and it is needless to say that it is furnished with every comfort and luxury. The library opens into this room, and I had to pass out from where I was sitting into this library and get upon a chair to reach the volumes I wanted to examine. There were six small volumes in all. I took them down and placed them at my right hand in a little pile, and set to work – sometimes reading, sometimes writing. As I finished with a book I placed it in front of me. There were four silver candlesticks upon the table, the candles all burning and, as I am a chilly person, I sat myself at one corner of the table with the fire on my left, and at intervals, as I had finished with a book, I rose, knocked the fire together and stood up to warm my feet. I continued in this way at my task till nearly one o'clock. I had got on better than I had expected and had only one more book to occupy me. I rose, wound up my watch, and opened a bottle of Seltzer water, and I remember thinking to myself that I should get to bed by two after all. I set to work on the last little book. I had been engaged upon it about half an hour, and was just beginning to think that my task was drawing to a close, when, *as I was actually writing*, I saw a large white hand within a foot of my elbow. Turning my head, there sat a figure of a somewhat large man, with his back to the fire, bending slightly over the table, and apparently examining the pile of books that I had been at work upon. The man's face was turned away from me, but I saw his closely cut, reddish-brown hair, his ear and shaved cheek, the eyebrow, the corner of the right eye, the side of the forehead, and the large high cheek-bone. He was dressed in what I can only describe as a kind of ecclesiastical habit of thick corded silk or some such material, close up to the throat, and a narrow trim or edging, of about an inch broad, of satin or velvet serving as a stand-up collar, and fitting close to the chin. The right hand, which had first attracted my attention, was clasping, without any great pressure, the left hand; both hands were in perfect repose, and the light blue veins of the right hand were conspicuous. I remember thinking that the hand was like the hand of Velasquez's magnificent 'Dead Knight', in the National Gallery. I looked at my visitor for some seconds, and was perfectly sure that he was not a reality. A thousand thoughts came crowding upon me, but not the least feeling of alarm, or even uneasiness; curiosity and a strong interest were uppermost. For an instant I felt eager to make a sketch of my friend, and I looked at a tray on my right for a pencil; then I thought, 'Up-stairs I have a sketch-book – shall I fetch it?' There he sat, and I was fascinated; afraid not of his staying, but *lest he should go*. Stopping in my writing, I lifted my left hand from the paper, stretched it out to the pile of books, and moved the top one. I cannot explain why I did this – my arm passed in front of the figure, and it vanished. I was simply disappointed and nothing more. I went on with my writing as if nothing had happened, perhaps for another five minutes, and I had actually got to the last few words of what I had determined to extract when the figure appeared again, exactly in the same place and attitude as before. I saw the hands close to my own; I turned my head again to examine him more closely, and I was framing a sentence to address him when I discovered that I did not dare to speak. I was afraid of the sound of my own voice. There he sat, and there sat I. I turned my head again to my work, and finished writing the two or three words I still had to write. The paper and my notes are at this moment before me, and exhibit not the slightest tremor or nervousness. I could point out the words I was writing when the phantom came, and when he disappeared. Having finished my task, I shut the book, and threw it on the table; it made a slight noise as it fell – the figure vanished.

Throwing myself back in my chair, I sat for some seconds looking at the fire with a curious mixture of feeling, and I remember wondering whether my friend would come again, and if he did whether he would hide the fire from me. Then first there stole upon me a dread and a suspicion that I was beginning to lose my nerve. I remember yawning; then I rose, lit my bedroom candle, took my books into the inner library, mounted the chair as before, and replaced five of the volumes; the sixth I brought back and laid upon the table where I had been writing when the phantom did me the honour to appear to me. By this time I had lost all sense of uneasiness. I blew out the four candles and marched off to bed, where I slept the sleep of the just or the guilty – I know not which – but I slept very soundly.

This is a simple and unvarnished narrative of facts. Explanation, theory, or inference, I leave to others.

Jessopp, *Frivola*, pp. 7–15.

53
The Man-Monkey

Charlotte Burne, whose account is reproduced here, says that this 'very weird story of an encounter with an animal ghost arose of late years' within her 'own knowledge'. Her informant for this version was 'Mr B— himself'.

The scene of the legend is actually quite a strange place. The cutting for the canal is unusually deep where Thomas Telford's turnpike road crosses it, and the bridge is of unusual construction, its height requiring that it should be braced with a double-decker arch. Both canal and bridge were of reasonably recent construction at the time the story of the Man-Monkey was current.

On 21 January 1879, a labouring man was employed to take a cart of luggage from Ranton in Staffordshire to Woodcote, beyond Newport, in Shropshire, for the use of a party of visitors who were going from one house to the other. He was late in coming back; his horse was tired, and could only crawl along at a foot's pace, so that it was ten o'clock at night when he arrived at the place where the highroad crosses the Birmingham and Liverpool Canal. Just before he reached the canal bridge, a strange black creature with great white eyes sprang out of the plantation by the road-side and alighted on his horse's back. He tried to push it off with his whip, but to his horror the whip went *through* the Thing, and he dropped it to the ground in his fright. The poor tired horse broke into a canter, and rushed onwards at full speed with the ghost still clinging to its back. How the creature at length vanished the man hardly knew. He told his tale in the village of Woodseaves, a mile further on, and so effectually frightened the hearers that one man actually stayed with his friends there all night, rather than cross the terrible bridge which lay between him and his home. The ghost-seer reached home at length, still in a state of excessive terror (but, as his master assured me, perfectly sober), and it was some days before he was able to leave his bed, so much was he prostrated by his fright. The whip was searched for next day, and found just at the place where he said he had dropped it.

Now comes the curious part of the story. The adventure, as was natural, was much talked of in the neighbourhood, and of course with all sorts of variations. Some days later the man's master (Mr B— of L—d) was surprised by a visit from a policeman, who came to request him to give information of his having been stopped and robbed on the Big Bridge on the night of the 21st January. Mr B— much amused, denied having been robbed, either on the canal bridge or anywhere else, and told the policeman the story just related. 'Oh, was that all, sir?' said the disappointed policeman. 'Oh, I know what *that* was. That was the Man-Monkey, sir, as *does* come again at that bridge ever since the man was drowned in the Cut.'

– Burne, *Shropshire Folklore*, pp. 106–07.

54
The Master Builder's Tale

Catherine Crowe's introduction to this story of a haunted house in London begins thus: 'I know of two or three other houses in this city, and one in the neighbourhood, in which circumstances of this nature are transpiring, or have transpired very lately; but people hush them up, from the fear of being laughed at, and also from an apprehension of injuring the character of a house, on which account I do not dwell on the particulars. But there was, some time since, a fama *of this kind attached to a house in J— Street, some of the details of which became very public.'*

Catherine Crowe (1800–76) was a writer, translator and novelist, the author of several best-sellers in the middle years of the century. The Night-Side of Nature *is generally regarded as a classic of psychical research.*

After telling of various hauntings in the house in J— Street, she continues the story as follows:

After this period the house was empty again for a considerable time, but was at length taken and workmen sent in to repair it. One day, when the workmen were away at dinner, the master tradesman took the key and went to inspect progress, and, having examined the lower room, he was ascending the stairs, when he heard a man's foot[step] behind him. He looked round, but there was nobody there, and he moved on again; still there was somebody following, and he stopped and looked over the rails; but there was no one to be seen. So, although feeling rather queer, he advanced into the drawing-room, where a fire had been lighted; and, wishing to combat the uncomfortable sensation that was creeping over him, he took hold of a chair, and drawing it resolutely along the floor, he slammed it down upon the hearth with some force and seated himself upon it; when, to his amazement, the action, in all its particulars of sound, was immediately repeated by his unseen companion, who seemed to seat himself. Horror-struck, the worthy builder started up and rushed out of the room.

– Crowe, *The Night-Side of Nature*, p. 275.

55
The Murder of Mr Perceval

On 11 May 1812 the Prime Minister of England, Spenser Perceval, was shot in the lobby of the House of Commons by a man with a grievance against the Government. It is the only assassination of a serving Prime Minister in British history. Perceval had been Prime Minister for three years, having previously (1807–09) served as Leader of the House of Commons and Chancellor of the Exchequer in the Duke of Portland's administration. The man who shot him was John Bellingham, a merchant who had been unjustly imprisoned in Russia and felt that the British Government owed him compensation for his sufferings and bankruptcy. His pleas had fallen on deaf ears. Bellingham made no attempt to escape or to deny his crime. He was tried, found guilty and executed in public.

The story of how a Cornish squire saw the murder in a dream has been much anthologised. It may be found in several sources including John Ingram's The Haunted Homes and Family Traditions of Great Britain *(pp. 224–27) and Sabine Baring-Gould's* Cornish Characters and Strange Events *(pp. 427–31). The two most interesting accounts, however, come from Frederick George Lee and Andrew Lang.*

Lee says that this story was 'exceedingly well authenticated' by his own aunt. His account in The Other World *(pp. 226–30) ends with the aunt's sworn testimony, written down in May 1873. Lang's version (quoted below) is a first-person account from the dreamer himself, dated 1832. In both of these accounts the dreamer mis-identifies Mr Perceval not as the current Prime Minister but in his former role as Chancellor of the Exchequer.*

The drawing which Mr Williams used to identify the Prime Minister was printed in the Newgate Calendar, *and may be seen (rather blurred) in the Wikipedia entry on the murder.*

'SUNDHILL, December, 1832.

'[Some account of a dream which occurred to John Williams, Esq., of Scorrier House, in the county of Cornwall, in the year 1812. Taken from his own mouth, and narrated by him at various times to several of his friends.]

'Being desired to write out the particulars of a remarkable dream which I had in the year 1812, before I do so I think it may be proper for me to say that at that time my attention was fully occupied with affairs of my own – the superintendence of some very extensive mines in Cornwall being entrusted to me. Thus I had no leisure to pay any attention to political matters, and hardly knew at that time who formed the administration of the country. It was, therefore, scarcely possible that my own interest in the subject should have had any share in suggesting the circumstances which presented themselves to my imagination. It was, in truth, a subject which never occurred to my waking thoughts.

'My dream was as follows:

'About the second or third day of May, 1812, I dreamed that I was in the lobby of the House of Commons (a place well known to me). A small man, dressed in a blue coat and a white waistcoat, entered, and immediately I saw a person whom I had observed on my first entrance, dressed in a snuff-coloured coat with metal buttons, take a pistol from under his coat and present it at the little man above-mentioned. The pistol was discharged, and the ball entered under the left breast of the person at whom it was directed. I saw the blood issue from the place where the ball had struck him, his countenance instantly altered, and he fell to the ground. Upon inquiry who the sufferer might be, I was informed that he was the chancellor. I understood him to be Mr Perceval, who was Chancellor of the Exchequer. I further saw the murderer laid hold of by several of the gentlemen in the room. Upon waking I told the particulars above related to my wife; she treated the matter lightly, and desired me to go to sleep, saying it was only a dream. I soon fell asleep again, and again the dream presented itself with precisely the same circumstances. After waking a second time and stating the matter again to my wife, she only repeated her request that I would compose myself and dismiss the subject from my mind. Upon my falling asleep the third time, the same dream without any alteration was repeated, and I awoke, as on the former occasions, in great agitation. So much alarmed and impressed was I with the circumstances above related, that I felt much doubt whether it was not my duty to take a journey to London and communicate upon the subject with the party principally concerned. Upon this point I consulted with some friends whom I met on business at the Godolphin mine on the following day. After having stated to them the particulars of the dream itself and what were my own feelings in relation to it, they dissuaded me from my purpose, saying I might expose myself to contempt and vexation, or be taken up as a fanatic. Upon this I said no more, but anxiously watched the newspapers every evening as the post arrived.

'On the evening of the 13th of May (as far as I recollect) no account of Mr Perceval's death was in the newspapers, but my second son, returning from Truro, came in a hurried manner into the room where I was sitting and exclaimed: "O father, your dream has come true! Mr Perceval has been shot in the lobby of the House of Commons; there is an account come from London to Truro written after the newspapers were printed."

'The fact was Mr Perceval was assassinated on the evening of the 11th.

'Some business soon after called me to London, and in one of the print-shops I saw a drawing for sale, representing the place and the circumstances which attended Mr Perceval's death. I purchased it, and upon a careful examination I found it to coincide in all respects with the scene which had passed through my imagination in the dream. The colours of the dresses, the buttons of the assassin's coat, the white waistcoat of Mr Perceval, the spot of blood upon it, the countenances and attitudes of the parties present were exactly what I had dreamed.

'The singularity of the case, when mentioned among my friends and acquaintances, naturally made it the subject of conversation in London, and in consequence my friend, the late Mr Rennie, was requested by some of the commissioners of the navy that they might be permitted to hear the circumstances from myself. Two of them accordingly met me at Mr Rennie's house, and to them I detailed at the time the particulars, then fresh in my memory, which form the subject of the above statement.

'I forbear to make any comment on the above narrative, further than to declare solemnly that it is a faithful account of facts as they actually occurred. (Signed) JOHN WILLIAMS.'

– Lang, *The Book of Dreams and Ghosts*, pp. 36–42.

56
Old Nanny's Ghost

T. F. Thiselton-Dyer, whose account is quoted below, attributes this legend to Henderson's Folklore of the Northern Counties *and describes it as 'the history of an apparition which, with retributive justice, once haunted a certain Yorkshire farmer'.*

Stokesley is a small market town on the River Leven in North Yorkshire, 10 miles south of Middlesborough.

An old woman of Sexhow, near Stokesley, appeared after her death to a farmer of the place, and informed him that beneath a certain tree in his apple orchard he would find a hoard of gold and silver which she had buried there; the silver he was to keep for his trouble, but the gold he was to give to a niece of hers living in great poverty. The farmer went to the spot indicated, found the money, and kept it all to himself. But from that day his conscience gave him no rest, and every night, at home or abroad, Old Nanny's ghost dogged his steps. At last one evening the neighbours heard him returning from Stokesley Market very late; his horse was galloping furiously, and as he passed a neighbour's house, its inmates heard him screaming out, 'I will, I will, I will!' But when the horse reached the farm all was still, for the rider was a corpse.

– Thiselton-Dyer, *The Ghost World*, p. 399.

57
Old Sykes's Wife

This very well-known Lancashire legend has appeared in some form in most collections of folklore from the North of England, in works by regional authors (e.g. William Dobson's Rambles by the Ribble, *1883), and in several more general anthologies too (e.g. Ingram's* Haunted Homes and Family Traditions of Great Britain, *and T. F. Thiselton-Dyer's* The Ghost World). *The version given below comes from Harland and Wilkinson's* Legends and Traditions of Lancashire *of 1873. For another, equally famous, Samlesbury ghost in Harland and Wilkinson's collection, see story no. 69, 'The White Lady of Samlesbury'.*

In her Haunted England *of 1940, folklorist Christina Hole (1896–1985) says that she had stayed at 'the modern Sykes Lumb' some years previously and 'found there was a vague local belief that the cottage was still haunted though the present owner had never seen or heard anything supernatural'. Though the supposed events are dated to the period just after the Wars of the Roses (1455–85), I have found no trace of the story in ghost literature before the mid-nineteenth century. Modern paranormal databases record no contemporary stories or sightings.*

In a secluded dell, on the banks of Mellor Brook, not far from the famous Old Hall of Samlesbury, stands a lonely farmhouse which was occupied for many generations by a family named Sykes. They gave their name to the homestead, or *vice versa*, on its being cleared from the forest; and from the fact of pastures lying at a short distance from a broad and deep portion of the brook, it became generally known by the name of Sykes Lumb Farm. The Sykes, however, have long since become extinct; but the doings of one of the race have passed into tradition, and will, no doubt, be handed down to many future generations.

It is said that one of the latest occupants of the farm had become very rich, partly by the constant hoarding of his ancestors, partly from the thrift of his too-covetous wife, but much more by having discovered the hidden treasures of some former possessor. Be that as it may, civil troubles arose, and the Wars of the Roses exhausted not only the wealth but the population of Lancashire. Old Sykes's wife had neither son nor daughter. Her husband was too old to be called off to the wars; and hence her only anxiety was lest some lawless marauders should seize upon their stores. She had, besides, no notion of becoming dependent upon the bounty of the Southworths of the Hall, nor did she relish the idea of soliciting charity at the gates of the lordly Abbot of Whalley. Her treasure was therefore carefully secured in earthenware jars, and was then buried deep beneath the roots of an apple tree in the orchard. Years passed away, and the troubles of the country did not cease...

But e're peace blessed the land, Old Sykes had paid the debt of nature, and left his wife the sole possessor of their buried wealth. She, too, soon passed away; and, as the legend asserts, so suddenly that she had no opportunity to disclose the place where she had deposited her treasure. Rumour had not failed to give her the credit of being possessed of considerable wealth; but, although her relatives made diligent search, they were unsuccessful in discovering the place of the hidden jars. The farm passed into other hands, and Old Sykes's wife might have been forgotten had not her ghost, unable to find rest, continued occasionally to visit the old farmhouse.

Many a time, in the dusk of the evening, have the neighbouring peasants met an old wrinkled woman dressed in ancient garb, passing along the gloomy road which leads across the Lumb, but fear always prevented them from speaking. She never lifted her head, but helped herself noiselessly along, by means of a crooked stick, which bore no resemblance to those then in use. At times she was seen in the old barn, on other occasions in the house, but more frequently in the orchard, standing by an apple tree which still flourished over the place where the buried treasure was afterwards said to have been found. Generations passed away, and still her visits continued. One informant minutely described her withered visage, her short quaintly-cut gown, her striped petticoat, and her stick. He was so much alarmed that he ran away from the place, notwithstanding that he had engaged to perform some urgent work. 'She was not there,' he gravely said, 'when I went to pluck an apple, but no sooner did I raise my hand towards the fruit, than she made her appearance just before me.' At last, it is said, an occupier of the farm, when somewhat elated by liquor, ventured to question her as to the reasons for her visits. She returned no answer, but after moving slowly towards the stump of an old apple-tree, she pointed significantly towards a portion of the orchard which had never been disturbed.

On search being made, the treasure was found deep down in the earth, and as the soil was being removed, the venerable-looking shade was seen standing on the edge of the trench. When the last jar was lifted out, an unearthly smile passed over her withered features; her bodily form became less and less distinct, until at last it disappeared altogether. Since then the old farmhouse has ceased to be haunted. Old Sykes's wife is believed to have found eternal rest; – but there are yet many, both old and young, who walk with quickened step whenever they are belated, fearful lest they should be once more confronted with the dreaded form of its unearthly visitor.

– Harland and Wilkinson, *Legends and Traditions of Lancashire*, pp. 55–57.

58
Padfoot

This legend is one of very many stories in British folklore about threatening ghostly animals, especially the fearsome 'Black Dogs' that are said to accost travellers in lonely places.

In Yorkshire, the villages around Leeds have a nocturnal terror called the Padfoot. He is described as about the size of a small donkey, black, with shaggy hair and large eyes like saucers; and it follows people by night, or waylays them in the road which they have to pass.

A certain Yorkshire woman, called Old Sally Dransfield, the carrier from Leeds to Swillington, is a firm believer in the Padfoot. She declares that she has often seen it – sometimes rolling along the ground before her, like a woolpack – sometimes vanishing suddenly through a hedge.

My friend, the Rev. J. C. Atkinson speaks of the Padfoot as a precursor of death; as sometimes visible, sometimes invisible, but ever and anon padding lightly in the rear of people, then again before them or at their side, and uttering a roar totally unlike the voice of any known animal. Sometimes the trail of a chain would be heard, accompanying the light quick pad of the feet. In size it was somewhat larger than a sheep, with long smooth hair. It was certainly safer to leave the creature alone, for a word or a blow gave it power over you; and a story is told of a man, whose way being obstructed again and again by the Padfoot, kicked the thing, and was forthwith dragged along through hedge and ditch to his home, and left under his own window.

A man in Horbury has lately seen 'the Padfoot'. He was going home and he saw a white dog in the hedge. He struck at it, and the stick passed through it. Then the white dog looked at him, and it had 'great saucer e'en'; and he was so 'flayed' that he ran home trembling and went to bed, when he fell ill and died. The Padfoot, in this neighbourhood, is a white dog like a 'flay-craw'. It goes sometimes on two legs, sometimes it runs on three. To see it is a prognostication of death.

– Henderson, *Folklore of the Northern Counties*, pp. 237–38.

59
The Red Barn

Frederick George Lee prefaces this account of a famous murder with these remarks: 'The number of records in which it is believed that dreams have been the means by which murder has been discovered are so considerable; and some are so well authenticated, that it is impossible, as it certainly would be presumptuous, to endeavour to set them aside. The murder of Maria Marten of Polstead in Suffolk, by William Corder, a farmer, in May of the year 1827, is a remarkable example.'

The trial occasioned huge local interest. While Corder was still in custody plays were being acted before eager audiences, ballad singers were performing songs, and an exhibition depicting scenes of the murder was staged at Polstead Fair less than a month before the trial. There was also a thriving market for souvenirs; the Red Barn was plundered by souvenir hunters, who removed the boards to a height of 5–6 feet.

According to information on the website of St Edmondsbury District Council, the only known remaining relics are a wooden shoe-shaped snuff box – now in Moyse's Hall collection – and an iron stay from the barn doors in a private collection. (See http://www.stedmundsbury.gov.uk/sebc/visit/theindustry.cfm).

[Maria Marten] was induced to leave her home [accompanying William Corder] the man who, under the promise of marriage, had betrayed her [and having been taken] to a certain barn, was there cruelly murdered and buried under the floor. For nearly twelve months the murder was undiscovered; for Corder, who remained away, but still communicated with her parents, maintained that she had married him; that circumstances prevented his bringing her back to his father's home: but that in due course they would both come, though it was implied that they were both on the Continent.

The mother of the murdered woman, however, about ten months after her daughter's death, dreamed that her daughter had been murdered, and buried under the floor of the [Red Barn]. So strong and deep an impression did this make both on her relations and the people of the village, that the girl's father and others on 19 April 1828, took up the floor of the barn, where they discovered the body of the murdered woman in a sack; and not so much decayed but that obvious marks of violence were perceptible. The body was successfully identified by the want of two teeth – one on the left side of the upper jaw, and the other on the right side of the lower. In the meantime Corder had married, and had gone to live in Essex, where he was apprehended, tried, and condemned on the strongest circumstantial evidence. He made a full confession of the murder when in prison, under sentence of death, and was executed in August, 1828.

– Lee, *The Other World; Or, Glimpses of the Supernatural*, pp. 230–31.

60
The Roaring Bull of Bagbury

In introducing this story, the prolific Shropshire folklore collector and writer, Charlotte Burne, remarked that although the Roaring Bull had been 'laid' for generations, 'the affair was still talked of in Bishop's Castle and all along the Shropshire side of the Welsh Border'.

Hyssington, 10 miles south of Welshpool, 'the scene of his conquest by the assembled parsons,' she says, 'is a parish partly in Shropshire and partly in Montgomeryshire ... [The story] was taken down in 1881 from the narration of an old farmer named Hayward.'

Hyssington is clearly proud of its legend. A booklet entitled The Roaring Bull of Bagbury: A Legend and its Story *is for sale in the church. This gives an alternative version of the legend with a 'prequel' in which the villagers, exhausted by the depredations of the cruel squire, ask a witch to help them; the witch's curse backfires and turns the squire into a bull after his death.*

Above the book-stall, there is a painting of the exorcism scene showing a large but quite friendly-looking pink bull and two men in Jacobean costume, one reading from a Prayer Book, the other holding a candle.

The church lies some distance from the village next to an ancient earthworks (motte-and-bailey construction), and is dedicated to St Etheldreda, the only such dedication in Wales (though there is another St Etheldreda's in London). It was extensively restored in 1875, so it is no longer possible to see the damage to the west end that the bull was supposed to have inflicted.

The story is very similar to 'The Great Giant of Henllys' (story no. 26), and Ella Leather's story of Black Vaughan from the other side of the Welsh/ English border (see The Folklore of Herefordshire*). It is a classic 'migratory legend'.*

There was a very bad man lived at Bagbury Farm, and when he died it was said that he had never done but two good things in his life, and the one was to give a waistcoat to a poor old man, and the other was to give a piece of bread and cheese to a poor boy, and when this man died he made a sort of confession of this. But when he was dead his ghost would not rest, and he would get in the buildings in the shape of a bull, and roar till the boards and the shutters and the tiles would fly off the building, and it was impossible for anyone to live near him. He never came till about nine or ten at night, but he got so rude at last that he would come about seven or eight at night, and he was so troublesome that they sent for twelve parsons to lay him. And the parsons came, and they got him under, but they could not lay him; but they got him, in the shape of a bull all the time, up into Hyssington Church. And when they got him into the church, they all had candles, and one old blind parson, who knowed him, and knowed what a rush he would make, he carried his candle in his top boot. And he made a great rush, and all the candles went out, all but the blind parson's, and he said, 'You light your candles by mine.' And while they were in the church, before they laid him, the bull made such a burst that he cracked the wall of the church from the top to the bottom, and the crack was left as it was for years, till the church was done up; it was left on purpose for people to see. I've seen it hundreds of times.

Well, they got the bull down at last, into a snuff-box, and he asked them to lay him under Bagbury Bridge, and that every mare passed over should lose her foal, and every woman her child; they would not do this, and they laid him in the Red Sea for a thousand years.

I remember the old clerk at Hyssington. He was an old man sixty years ago, and he told me he could remember the old parson well.

But long after the ghost had been laid in the Red Sea, 'folk were always frightened to go over Bagbury Bridge,' said John Thomas. 'I've bin over it myself many a time with horses, and I always got off the horse and made him go quietly, and went pit-pat, ever so softly, for fear of *him* hearing me and coming out.'

– Burne, *Shropshire Folklore*, pp. 107–09.

61
Short-Hoggers of Whittinghame

This amusing legend can also be found in Katharine Briggs's mammoth work, A Dictionary of British Folk-Tales in the English Language, part B, Folk Legends, *vol. 1, p. 566. She quotes its source as below.*

It is supposed to be not yet a century since the good people of Whittinghame got happily quit of a ghost, which, in the shape of an 'unchristened wean' [unbaptised child] had annoyed them for many years. An unnatural mother having murdered her child at a large tree, not far from the village, the ghost of the deceased was afterward seen, on dark nights, running in a distracted manner between the said tree and the churchyard, and was occasionally heard crying. The villagers believe that it was obliged to take the air, and bewail itself, on account of wanting a name – no anonymous person, it seems, being able to get a proper footing in the other world. Nobody durst speak to the unhappy little spirit from a superstitious dread of dying immediately after; and, to all appearance, the village of Whittinghame was destined to be haunted till the end of time, for want of an exorcist. At length it fortunately happened that a drunkard, one night on reeling home, encountered the spirit, and, being fearless in the strength of John Barleycorn, did not hesitate to address it in the same familiar style as if it had been one of his own flesh-and-blood fellow topers.

'How's a' wi' ye this morning, Short-Hoggers?' cried the courageous villager; when the ghost immediately ran away, joyfully exclaiming:

'O weel's me noo, I've gotten a name;
They ca' me Short-Hoggers o' Whittinghame.'

And since that time it has never been either seen or heard of.

– Chambers, *The Popular Rhymes of Scotland*, p. 334.

62
Silky of Black Heddon

This version of a famous local legend can be found in William Henderson's Folklore of the Northern Counties. *There is a slightly earlier account in M. A. Richardson's* The Local Historian's Table Book of Remarkable Occurrences

(London, 1841–46) and later versions in collections such as those of John Ingram 1884, T. F. Thiselton-Dyer 1893 and Christina Hole 1940. This version has been chosen for its delightful literary style, but nevertheless it is genuinely a product of the oral tradition. It is full of folk motifs such as the power of ghosts to stop horses, guard treasure, and foretell a death; also, as Henderson remarks, some of Silky's antics also resemble those of brownies and other household spirits.

Belsay Hall, Castle and Gardens, near Morpeth, Northumberland are in the care of English Heritage and open to the public.

About eighty or ninety years ago, the quiet village of Black Heddon, near Stamfordham, in Northumberland, was greatly disturbed by a supernatural being, popularly called Silky, from the nature of her robes. She was remarkable for the suddenness with which she would appear to benighted travellers, breaking forth upon them, in dazzling splendour, in the darkest and most lonely parts of the road. If he were on horseback, she would seat herself behind him, 'rustling in her silks', accompany him a certain distance, and then as suddenly disappear, leaving the bewildered countryman in blank amazement.

Silky had a favourite resort at Belsay, two or three miles from Black Heddon, on a romantic crag beautifully studded with trees, under whose shadow she would wander all night. The bottom of this crag is washed by a picturesque little lake, at whose outlet is a water-fall, over which a fine old tree spreads its waving branches, forming by their intersection a sort of chair. In this Silky loved to sit, rocked to repose by the wild winds, and it is still called Silky's Chair; Sir Charles M. L. Monck, the present proprietor of the place, preserving the tree carefully, on account of the legend.

This sprite exercised a marvellous power over the brute creation, arresting horses in their daily work, and keeping them still as long as she was so minded. Once she waylaid a waggon bringing coals to a farm near Black Heddon, and fixed the team upon a bridge, since called, after her, 'Silky's Brig'. Do what he would, the driver could not make the horses move a step, and there they would have stood all night had not another farm servant fortunately come up with some 'witchwood' (mountain-ash) about him. He went to the horses, and they moved on at once, but never did their driver dare to go abroad again without being well armed with witchwood.

In some respects Silky showed a family likeness to the Brownies. Like them she would, during the night, tidy a disorderly house; but if cannie decent people had cleaned their rooms, and arranged them neatly, especially on a Saturday afternoon, the wayward sprite would disarrange everything as soon as they were gone to bed, so that on Sunday morning all would be in the wildest confusion.

Silky disappeared from her haunts very suddenly. One day a female servant, being alone in one of the rooms of a house at Black Heddon, was terribly frightened by the ceiling above suddenly giving way, and a black mass falling through it with a crash upon the floor. She instantly fled out of the room, screaming at the pitch of her voice, 'The devil's in the house! The devil's in the house! He's come through the ceiling!' The family collected around her in some alarm, and at first no one dared enter the room; when the mistress at last ventured to go in, she found on the floor a large rough skin filled with gold. From this time Silky was never more heard or seen, so it was believed that she was the troubled phantom of some person who had died miserable because she owned treasure, and was overtaken by her mortal agony before she had disclosed its hiding-place.

The Rev. J. F. Bigge relates, however, that an old woman named Pearson, of Welton Mill, whom he visited on her deathbed, told him, a few days before her death, that she had seen Silky the night before, sitting at the bottom of her bed, all dressed in silk.

– Henderson, *Folklore of the Northern Counties*, pp. 230–32.

63
A Spectral Funeral

'The most veritable ghost,' writes Mrs Eliza Gutch introducing this story from North Yorkshire, 'was the one which was supposed to be the ghost of Archbishop Scrope, who for many years walked the road to conduct his own funeral procession.'

Richard le Scrope (c. 1350–1405) was Archbishop of York under Richard II, the Yorkist king who, in 1399, was overthrown by the Lancastrian nobleman Henry Bolingbroke who became Henry IV. Scrope was deeply involved in plots against the new king, openly supporting the king's enemies and preaching against him in the Minster. At the end of May 1405, Archbishop Scrope found himself at the head of an army of 8,000 men, facing a large loyalist army on Shipton Moor. Scrope disbanded his force in exchange for a truce but was immediately arrested. Henry himself travelled to York for the trial; the Archbishop was found guilty of treason, and beheaded outside the city walls of York.

The Palace of the Archbishop of York is at Bishopsthorpe. A modern stained-glass window, one of three depicting local scenes and historical events in the nearby church of St Andrew, depicts Archbishop Scrope accompanied by armed soldiers coming before King Henry IV at his trial.

'Perhaps the most persistent story told of his appearance,' Mrs Gutch continues, 'was that told by a man who made his living as a slaughterman. He used to speak with confidence of what he saw.' This is the slaughterman's story ...

This Robert Johnson, accompanied by a boy who was apprenticed to a Jubbergate butcher, was sent one night to a farm beyond Bishopsthorpe to fetch some sheep. As they returned in the darkness, nearing the hauling lane, each suddenly saw a coffin suspended in the air, and moving slowly along in the direction of York. It tilted occasionally, as if borne on the shoulders of men who were thrown out of step by the rugged character of the roadway. The coffin was covered with a heavy black pall of velvet, fringed with white silk, and was in size and appearance the resting-place of a full-grown man. Behind it, with measured tread, walked a Bishop in lawn, bearing on his hands a large open book, over which his head bent, but from his lips no sound came. On went the procession, with the steady precision observed in bearing the dead to the grave, whilst the sheep kept pace, and would not be driven past the strange sight. Nobody could be mistaken in the apparition. The night, though dark, was too light to admit of mistake. The spectre procession moved at a leisured pace for some considerable distance till it came to the field where the Archbishop was beheaded. Then it disappeared as hastily as it had come, and returned to its rest. But not so with the man and boy. Having arrived at their destination after very few particulars, spoken amid much fear, they were taken off to bed, where they remained for many days, wrung in mind and body by the terrible shock. When sufficiently recovered, their story was repeated with particular detail, and gained universal credence, from the fact many villagers and many citizens had experienced like sight and sensation. The boy forsook his business and took to the sea, lest he should ever again be compelled to take a similar journey, and be subject to like experience, whilst the man ever after avoided that road at nightfall, but never swerved from declaring his story true. More than once after this, men who had sat late at their cups were frightened into sobriety by the reappearance of the strange funeral procession, but the ghost has done its work, for in our day it never appears.

– Gutch, *Examples of Printed Folklore Concerning the North Riding of Yorkshire*, pp. 93–94.

64
St Mary's Place, Stamford

This incident was reported in the Stamford & Rutland Guardian *on 26 March 1897. My thanks to Martin Smith for this item.*

The excitement of the week has centred round St Mary's Place, where it is said there is a 'haunted' house. For a long time past, indeed ever since the tenant entered into possession (four years ago), strange, unpleasant and unaccountable noises have been heard in the house, generally between the hours of eleven at night and four in the morning, and so seriously has this state of things affected the tenant's family, that last Friday he moved his furniture to another house. Ever since then the house has been the centre of attraction, and in the evenings crowds have waited in the hope of seeing or hearing something of a ghostly nature. On Tuesday morning, a gentleman who is an unbeliever in ghosts saw an apparition pass twice in front of the upstairs windows. He hastened to the house and on enquiry found that the only occupants were a servant girl and a washerwoman, and both were engaged downstairs. A search was immediately made of the house, but nothing was discovered.

From what we can gather, the noises which have been heard resemble a woman moaning and a man scolding, and on many occasions footsteps have been heard on the stairs repeatedly during the night, while the catches on the bedroom doors have been sounded and the doors opened. So great had the annoyance become, the servant girls could not be induced to go to bed, and the children manifested the greatest alarm and nervousness. On Friday night the whole of the upstairs windows were fastened, and we are informed by the gentleman who fastened them that, notwithstanding the fact that the house was tenantless and locked up, they were all wide open the following morning ...

We understand that two of local clergy are anxious to pass a night in the house in order to get on speaking terms, if possible, with a visitor from the other world.

– Smith, *Stamford Myths and Legends*, pp. 70–71.

65
Tommy and the Ghost

A shortened version of this story may be found in Katharine Briggs's mammoth work, A Dictionary of British Folk-Tales in the English Language, part B, Folk Legends, *vol. 1, pp. 592–93. Here it is given in its original form as published in the* Folklore Record *in 1879.*

There lived in the town of —, in that part of England which lies towards the borders of Wales, a very curious simple kind of a man; though, simple as he seemed, people all said there was more cunning in him than there appeared to be, and that he knew a good deal that other people did not know.

Now there was in the same town a certain large and very old house, and one of the rooms was haunted by a ghost, which not only hindered people from making any use of that room, but was also very troublesome to them in other ways. The man whom I have just mentioned was reported to be very clever at dealing with ghosts, and the proprietor of the haunted house, by the advice of some of his friends, sent for him and asked him if he would undertake to make the ghost quit the house.

Tommy, for that was the name the man generally went by, agreed to do this, on condition that he should have with him in the room which the ghost frequented three things, an empty bottle, a bottle of brandy with a tumbler, and a pitcher of water.

So Tommy had a fine fire in the room, for it was a cold winter evening, and he locked the door safely in the inside and sat down to pass the night drinking brandy and water.

Well, just as the clock struck twelve, he was roused by a slight noise, and looking up, lo! there was the ghost standing before him.

Says the ghost, 'Well, Tommy, how are ye?'

'Pretty well, thank ye,' says he, 'but, pray how did ye know my name?'

'Oh, very well indeed,' said the ghost.

'And how did ye get in?'

'Oh, very easily.'

'Not through the door, I'm sure.'

'No, not at all, but through the key-hole.'

'D'ye say so? none of your tricks upon me; I won't believe you came through the key-hole.'

'Won't ye? But I did.'

'I'm sure you can't get through the key-hole.'

'I'm sure I can.'

'Well, then,' says Tommy, pointing to the empty bottle, which he pretended to have emptied, 'if you can come through the key-hole you can get into this bottle, but I won't believe you can do either.'

Now the ghost began to be very angry that Tommy should doubt his powers of getting into the bottle, so he confidently asserted that it was easy to be done.

'No,' said Tommy, 'I won't believe it till I see you get in.'

'Here goes, then,' said the ghost, and sure enough into the bottle he went, and Tommy corked him up quite tight, so that he could not get out, and he took the bottle to the bridge where the river was wide and deep, and he threw the bottle exactly over the key-stone of the middle arch into the river, and the ghost was never heard of after.

– Thoms, 'The Laying of the Ghost'.

66
Tregeagle

This story is perhaps the most famous legend of Cornwall. It lays claim to some considerable antiquity, but it is not easily dated. Like John Ruddle (see story no. 7) and Parson Dodge (story no. 33), the legendary Tregeagle was a real person – or, strictly speaking in his case, an amalgam of several historical personages. According to the Ordnance Survey Leisure Map of Cornwall, *there were no fewer than five successive generations of John Tregeagles who were active in the sixteenth to eighteenth centuries in mid-Cornwall. The first was steward to Lord Robartes at Lanhydrock, and established a reputation as a severe magistrate. The second and third, his son and grandson, were Receivers General to the Duchy of Cornwall, and involved in a financial scandal.*

Besides his own variant, quoted below as 'Tregeagle 1', Robert Hunt records the existence of three other versions of this legend; one is in Cornish dialect ('Jahn Tergagle the Steward'); another ('Tregagle at Genvor Cove') features the well-known Cornish ghost-layer, Parson Corker; and the third, which he paraphrases rather than quotes, comes from 'Contemplation', a poem of 1807 by John Penwarne. I have been able to track this down and it is given here as 'Tregeagle 2'. For the folklorist the interest of this poem is the way Penwarne amalgamates the figure of Tregeagle with another Cornish tradition – the Dandy Dogs of Bodmin, relatives of the Wish Hounds of Dartmoor. Penwarne's attempt at 'antique' English is also noteworthy!

Tregeagle 1

Who has not heard of the wild spirit of Tregeagle? He haunts equally the moor, the rocky coasts, and the blown sandhills of Cornwall. From north to south, from east to west, this doomed spirit is heard of, and to the day of judgement he is doomed to wander, pursued by avenging fiends. For ever endeavouring to perform some task by which he hopes to secure repose, and being for ever defeated. Who has not heard the howling of Tregeagle? When the storms come with all their strength from the Atlantic, and urge themselves upon the rocks around Land's End, the howls of the spirit are louder than the roaring of the wind. When calms rest upon the ocean, and the waves can scarcely form upon the resting waters, low wailings creep along the coast. These are the wailings of this wandering soul. When midnight is on the moor or the mountains, and the night winds whistle among the rugged cairns, the shrieks of Tregeagle are distinctly heard [...]

There are some men who appear to be from their births given over to the will of tormenting demons. Such a man was Tregeagle ... Certain it is that the man Tregeagle was diabolically wicked. He seems to have been urged on from one crime to another until his cup of sin was overflowing ... At length death drew near to relieve the land of a monster whose name was a terror to all who heard it. Devils waited to secure the soul they had won, and Tregeagle in terror gave to the priesthood wealth, that they might fight with them and save his soul from eternal fire. Desperate was the struggle, but the powerful exorcisms of the banded brotherhood from a neighbouring monastery, drove back the evil ones, and Tregeagle slept with his fathers, safe in the custody of the churchmen, who buried him with high honours in St Breock Church ...

A dispute arose between two wealthy families respecting the ownership of extensive lands around Bodmin. The question had been rendered more difficult by the nefarious conduct of Tregeagle, who had acted as steward to one of the claimants, and who had destroyed ancient deeds, forged others, and indeed made it appear that he was the real proprietor of the domain ... A day was at length fixed, upon which a final decision must be come to ... The judge was about to sum up the case ... when the defendant ... proclaimed that he had another witness to produce. There was a strange silence in the judgement hall. It was felt that something chilling to the soul was amongst them, and there was a simultaneous throb of terror as Tregeagle was led into the witness box ...

The trial over, everyone expected to see the spectre-witness removed. There, however, he stood, powerless to fly, although he evidently desired to do so ...

'To bring him from the grave has been to me so dreadful a task, that I leave him in your care, and that of the Prior's ...' Having said this, the defendant left the court.

The churchmen were called in, and long were the deliberations between them and the lawyers, as to the best method of disposing of Tregeagle ... The only thing was to give him some task, difficult beyond the power of human nature, which might be extended far into eternity ...

One of the lawyers, remembering that Dozmary Pool was bottomless ... proposed that Tregeagle might be employed to empty this profound lake. Then one of the churchmen, to make the task more enduring, proposed that it should be performed with the aid of a limpet shell having a hole in it.

This was agreed to, and the required incantations were duly made. Bound by mystical spells, Tregeagle was removed to the dark moors and duly set to work. Year after year passed by, and there, day and night, summer and winter, storm and shine, Tregeagle was bending over the dark water, working hard with his perforated shell; yet the pool remained at the same level.

His old enemy the devil kept a careful eye on the doomed one, resolving, if possible, to secure so choice an example of evil. Often did he raise tempests sufficiently wild, as he supposed, to drive Tregeagle from his work, knowing that if he failed for a season to labour, he could seize and secure him. These were long tried in vain; but at length an auspicious hour presented itself.

Nature was at war with herself, the elements had lost their balance ... lightnings flashed ... fireballs fell ... thunders pealed ... an earthquake shook the solid earth ... the winds arose and raged with a fury that was irresistible, and hail beat so mercilessly on all things, that it spread death all around. Long did Tregeagle stand the pelting of the pitiless storm, but at length he yielded to its force and fled. The demons were in crowds at his heels [...]

Away, away went Tregeagle, faster and faster the dark spirits pursuing, and they had nearly overtaken him, when he saw Roach Rock and its chapel before him. He rushed up the rocks, with giant power clambered to the eastern window, and dashed his head through it, thus securing the shelter of its sanctity. The defeated demons retired, and long and loud were their wild wailings in the air. The inhabitants of the moors and of the neighbouring towns slept not a wink that night.

Tregeagle was safe, his head was within the holy church, though his body was exposed on a bare rock to the storm. Earnest were the prayers of the holy hermit in his cell on the rock to be relieved from his sinful visitor. In vain were the recluse's prayers. Day after day, as he knelt at the altar, the ghastly head of the doomed sinner grinned horridly down upon him ...

Things could not go on thus. The monks of Bodmin and the priests from the neighbouring churches gathered together, and the result of their long and anxious deliberations was, that Tregeagle, guarded by two saints, should be taken to the north coast, near Padstow, and employed making trusses of sand, and ropes of sand to bind them [...] The inhabitants of Padstow had seldom any rest. At every tide the howlings of Tregeagle banished sleep from each eye [and] people fled the town, and clustered upon the neighbouring plains praying, as with one voice, to be relieved from the sad presence of this monster.

St Petroc, moved by the tears and petitions of the people, resolved to remove the spirit; and by the intense earnestness of his prayers, after long wrestling, he subdued Tregeagle to his will. Having chained him with bonds ... every link of which had been welded with a prayer, St Petroc led the spirit away from the north coast, and stealthily placed him on the southern shores ... and there compelled him to carry sacks of sand across the estuary of the Loo, and to empty them at Porthleven, until the beach was clean down to the rocks. The priest was a good observer. He knew that the sweep of the tide [would carry the sand] back as steadily and speedily as fast as the spirit could move it. Long did Tregeagle labour; and, of course, in vain.

[But one day] Tregeagle was laden with a sack of sand of enormous size, and was wading across the mouth of the estuary, when one of the wicked devils [that pursued him still] tripped up the heavily-laden spirit. The sea was raging with the irritation of a passing storm; and, as Tregeagle fell, the sack was seized by the waves, and the contents poured out across this arm of the sea.

There, to this day, it rests a bar of sand, finally destroying the harbour ... The rage of the inhabitants of this sea-port – now destroyed – was great ... By the aid of the priests, and faith-inspired prayers, the bonds were once more placed on Tregeagle; and he was, by force of bell, book and candle sent to Land's End. There he would find no harbour to destroy or people to terrify. His task was to sweep the sands from Porthcurnow Cove round the headland called Tol-Peden-Penwith, into Nanjisal Cove. Those who know that rugged headland, with its cubical masses of granite, piled in Titanic grandeur one upon another, will appreciate the task; and when to all the difficulties are added the strong sweep of the Atlantic current ... it will be evident that the melancholy spirit has, indeed, a task which must endure until the world shall end.

Even until today is Tregeagle labouring at his task. In calms his wailing is heard; and those sounds which some call the 'soughing of the wind' are known to be the moanings of Tregeagle; whilst the coming storms are predicted by the fearful roarings of this condemned mortal.

– Hunt, *Popular Romances of the West of England*, pp. 132–38.

Tregeagle 2

In Cornwaile's fam'd land, bye the poole on the moore
   Tregeagle the wicked did dwelle;
He once was a shepherde contented and poore,
But growing ambitious and wishing for more,
   Sad fortune the shepherde befell.

One nyghte, all alone, as he cross'd the wylde heathe
   To drive his scant flocke to the folde,
All nature was stille, the wynds scarcely breathe
O'er the moone silver'd hilles and the vallies beneath,
   As he cast his eye over the wolde.

'Ah! Why sholde I live bye hard laboure' – quoth he,
   'And helde bye the rich in dysdayne!
'I wishe' – quoth TREGEAGLE – 'for all that I see,
'Oh then what a happye greate man I sholde be!
   When lorde of extensive domaine.'

Nowe scarce had he utter'd hys impious breath,
When the wolves they howl'd wildlye and loude;
The wyndes sadly syghing swept over the heath
As nature awoke from the styllness of deathe;
And the moone hyd her head in a cloude.

When suddaine he saw, midst the gloom of the nyghte,
A figure gygantick advance;
His hayre bristled up as he view'd the felle SPRYGHTE
Who seemed in form to be armed as a knyghte,
And he wielded an ebony lance.

All blacke was the gaunte steede on whych he dyd ryde;
A sable plume shadow'd his heade;
And blacke was his armoure, wyth bloode all bedy'de;
And blacke was the bugle that hung bye hys syde,
Which no mortale mighte hear without dread.

Two dogges fierce and felle, and whych never knew feare,
Did run hys fleete courser before;
Their forms were all hydeous, and grisly their haire,
And thro' their lanke sydes their sharpe ribs did appeare,
And their mouths were stille dripping with gore.

It is the devil, of course, who offers Tregeagle the usual deal; and time, of course, eventually runs out. Tregeagle tries to hide in his castle ...

All silente wythin, and the styllness of deathe
The darke frowning toweres surroundes;
When they heard, and eache – listenyng suspended his breath, –
They heard the shrill blaste from the farre dystaunte heath !
Whych the eares of all mortals confounds!

They hearde the BLACK HUNTER! and dreade shooke each mynde,
Heartes sanke that had never known feare;
The heard the BLACK HUNTER's dreade voyce in the wynde!
They hearde hys curste hell-houndes runn yelping behynde,
And his steede thundered loude on the eare!

And nowe he appear'd thro' the gloom of the nyghte;
Hys plume, seem'd a cloude in the skyes;
His forme the darke mists of the hylles to the syghte;
And as from a furnace shootes forth the rede lyghte,
Soe glared the fierce beams of hys eyes!

He blewe from hys bugle soe dreadeful a blaste,
Hys dogges howlyng hydeous the whyle,
That all NATURE trembled and shooke as aghaste!
And from the hygh walles the huge battlements braste!
Fell downe from the tottering pyle.

'Come forth SYR TREGEAGLE' – in thundere he cried,
'Come forth and submit to thy fate!
'Thy tyme is expired – to me thou arte tyde!
Wythyn thy dark castle in vayne thou wouldst hyde;
'Come forth! For here endeth thy date!'

Then forth came TREGEAGLE all palsyed with fear,
And fayne woulde more favoure have founde;
But loude roar'd the thundere, and swyfte thro' the ayre
The rede bolte of vengeaunce short forth wyth a glare,
And strooke hym a corpse to the grounde!

Then from the blacke corpse a pale SPECTRE appear'd,
And hyed him awaye thro' the nyghte,
When quickly the yelps of the hell houndes are hearde,
And to the pursuite bye the bugle are cheer'd,
Whyle behynde thunderes after the SPRYGHTE.

And nowe ruddy mornyng agayne gylds the skyes;
The hellyshe inchauntmente is o'er;
The forrests and castle no more meete theyre eyes;
But where from the greene woodes, its bryght turretes dyd rise,
Nowe spreades the darke poole on the moore.

[...]

And stylle, as the TRAV'LERE pursues hys lone waye
In horrour, at nyghts o'er the waste,

He heares SYR TREGEAGLE wyth shriekes rushe awaye,
He heares the BLACK HUNTER pursing hys preye,
And shrynkes at hys bugle's dreade blaste.

– Penwarne, *Contemplation*, pp. 93–136.

67
'Weep! Weep! Weep!'

This well-told story comes from Chapter 13 of Catherine Crowe's rambling portmanteau of a book, The Night-Side of Nature. *Chapter 13, which she entitles 'Haunted Houses', begins thus: 'Everybody has heard of haunted houses; and there is no country, and scarcely any place, in which something of the sort is not known or talked of; and I suppose there is no one who, in the course of their travels, has not seen very respectable, good-looking houses shut up and uninhabited, because they had this evil reputation assigned to them.' Chapter 13 contains eight or nine stories – legends and personal experience narratives – from around Europe, of which this is one.*

One of the most melancholy and impressive circumstances of this sort I have met with occurred to Mrs L—, a lady with whose family I am acquainted; Mrs L— herself having been kind enough to furnish me with the particulars: A few years since, she took a furnished house in Stevenson Street, North Shields, and she had been in it but a very few hours before she was perplexed by hearing feet in the passage, though, whenever she opened the door, she could see nobody. She went to the kitchen, and asked the servant if she had not heard the same sound. She said she had not, but there seemed to be strange noises in the house. When Mrs L— went to bed, she could not go to sleep for the noise of a child's rattle, which seemed to be inside her curtains. It rattled round her head, first on one side, then on the other; there were sounds of feet, and of a child crying, and a woman sobbing; and, in short, so many strange noises that the servant became frightened and went away. The next girl Mrs L— engaged came from Leith, and was a stranger to the place: but she had only passed a night in the house, when she said to her mistress, 'This is a troubled house you've got into, ma'am'; and she described, among the rest, that she had repeatedly heard her own name called by a voice near her, though she could see nobody.

One night Mrs L— heard a voice, like nothing human, close to her, cry, 'Weep! Weep! Weep!' Then there was a sound like some one struggling for breath, and again 'Weep! Weep! Weep!' then gasping, and a third time 'Weep! Weep!

Weep!' She stood still, and looked steadfastly on the spot from whence the voice proceeded, but could see nothing; and her little boy, who held her hand, kept saying 'What is that, mamma? What is that?' She describes the sound as most frightful. All the noises seemed to suggest the idea of childhood, and of a woman in trouble. One night, when it was crying round her bed, Mrs L— took courage, adjured it, upon which the noises ceased for that time, but there was no answer.

Mr L— was at sea when she took the house, and when he came home he laughed at the story at first, but soon became so convinced the account she gave was correct that he wanted to have the boards taken up, because, from the noises seeming to hover much about one spot, he thought perhaps some explanation of mystery might be found. But Mrs L— objected that if anything of a painful nature were discovered she should not be able to continue in the house, and as she must pay the year's rent, she wished, if possible, to make out the time.

She never saw anything but twice; once, the appearance of a child seemed to fall from the ceiling, close to her, and then disappear; and another time she saw a child run into a closet in a room at the top of the house; and it was most remarkable that a small door in that room, which was used for going out on to the roof, always stood open. However often they shut it, it was opened again immediately by an unseen hand, even before they got out of the room; and this continued the whole time they were in the house; while, night and day, some one in creaking shoes was heard pacing backward and forward in the room over Mr and Mrs L—'s heads.

At length the year expired; and to their great relief they quitted the house; but five or six years afterward, a person who had bought it, having taken up the floor of that upper room to repair it, there was found, close to the small door above alluded to, the skeleton of a child. It was then remembered that some years before a gentleman of somewhat dissolute habit had resided there, and that he was supposed to have been on very intimate terms with a young woman-servant who lived with him, but there had been no suspicion of anything more criminal.

– Crowe, *The Night-Side of Nature*, pp. 298–300.

68
The White Lady of Lewtrenchard

Lewtrenchard Manor, at Lewdown near Okehampton, Devon is now a smart hotel, but in earlier days it was the home of the Gould family, and is the setting for a famous 'White Lady' ghost story. The narrator of this version of the legend is a descendant of the family, the Revd Sabine Baring-Gould, an avid collector of folklore and legends, and the author of the famous hymn 'Onward, Christian

Soldiers'. Sabine Baring-Gould inherited the estate in 1872, undertaking a considerable renovation programme on the house between 1876 and 1913, and lived there with his wife and large family from 1881 onwards. He was Rector of St Peter's Lew Trenchard from 1881 to 1924. His grave is in the churchyard next to that of his wife Grace, a former mill-hand.

Apparently a woman of considerable courage and resourcefulness, his ancestor Madame Gould refused to go to bed in her last illness and died in her chair on 10 April 1795 (1796 according to a photocopied history of the house available at the manor). 'At the time of her death,' wrote folklorist Christina Hole in her Haunted England, *'all the shutters in the house flew open of themselves, and a farm-hand who came to find out the cause of the noise saw his dead mistress standing under a walnut tree in the garden.'*

Below is Sabine Baring-Gould's first-person account as told to William Henderson, author of Folklore of the Northern Counties.

Lewtrenchard House is haunted by a White Lady, who goes by the name of Madame Gould and is supposed to be the spirit of a lady who died there – like Queen Elizabeth, seated in her chair – in the middle of the last century. Her maiden name was Belfield, and she married William Drake Gould, son of Henry Gould and Elizabeth, only child of a Drake of Littleham.

Before the late alterations in Lew House, there was a corridor extending the whole length of the upper story of the house; along this the lady was supposed to walk at night, and her step was frequently heard.

My mother has often told me how she has heard the step at night, as though proceeding from high-heeled shoes, walking slowly up the corridor, and thinking it might be my father coming to bed, she has opened the door to admit him; but on looking out, she has seen the moon streaming in through the windows on an empty passage, down which she still heard the measured tread. My sister often expressed her desire to hear the steps of the spectral lady, but was still disappointed, though she sat up on purpose.

One summer night, however, she was sitting in her room, with window and door open, writing a letter, and thinking of anything but the old Madame, when she heard steps along the corridor. At the moment she thought it might be my father, and she rose, took up her candle, and went to the door to speak to him. To her surprise she saw no one, but the steps passed her, and went on into the lumber-room at the end of the passage. Being a resolute and courageous young lady, she followed the sound into the room, but could see no one. She also opened the only other door beyond her own, and which gave admittance to one of the servants' rooms, to ascertain whether the noise could have proceeded thence, but she found the two maids fast asleep.

At the end of the house is a long oak-tree avenue; the White Lady is said to have been seen pacing up and down this, gleaming in and out among the gnarled tree-trunks, as she passed into the moonlight or disappeared in the shade.

About three miles off is a quaint old granite mansion, half pulled down by my grandfather, and turned into a substantial farmhouse. The old hall, now converted into a granary, and reduced to half its original height, contains still a seven-light window, and three granite fireplaces. This ancient house belonged originally to the Woods, and there was a standing feud between that family and my own, till they were ruined, and Madame Gould bought the land and house from them; after which she declared she should die happy.

On the confines of this property, called Orchard, is a deep gloomy valley, through which trickles a rill of dark water, under the shadow of the thick fir plantations which clothe the sides of the glen. It goes by the name of the Black Valley, and the Bratton-Clovelly road plunges down into it, crosses a little bridge, and scrambles up the opposite side through the gloom of the over-hanging trees. On the side of the road is an old mine-shaft, long abandoned. It is confidently asserted by Lew and Bratton people that, on dark nights, Madame Gould is to be seen, dressed all in white, standing by the side of the stream, with a phosphorescent light streaming from her face and her clothes; and that she stoops and takes up handfuls of water, which she allows to trickle down in sparkling drops through her fingers. Sometimes she combs her long brown floating hair with a silver comb; and many a Bratton man, returning from market, has seen her and been nearly frightened out of his wits. Not many years ago, a man of that village had his leg broken by falling over a hedge, in his attempt to escape from the apparition, as it issued from the old mining-shaft and made towards him.

A young man, named Symmonds, living at a farm in the parish, left home for America during the old Madame's lifetime. After some years he returned, and hiring a horse at Tavistock, he rode home, a distance of twelve miles. It was a clear moonlight night, and as he passed through the Lew Valley, with the white rime lying thick on the grass, he noticed a newly-ploughed field, in which the plough had been left. On this was seated a lady in white satin, with long brown hair floating down her shoulders. Her face was up-lifted, and her eyes directed towards the moon, so that Mr Symmonds had a full view of it. He recognised her at once, and taking off his hat, he called out, 'I wish you a very good night, Madame.' She bowed in return, and waved her hand, the man noticing the sparkle of her diamond rings as she did so. On reaching home, after the first greetings and congratulations, he said to his aged parents, 'What do you think now? I have seen that strange Madame Gould sitting on a plough, this time o'night, and with frost on the ground, looking at the moon.' All who heard him started, and a blank expression passed over their countenances. The young man, seeing that he had surprised them more than he anticipated, asked what was the matter. The reply was, 'Madame was buried three days ago in Lew Church.'

– Henderson, *Folklore of the Northern Counties*, pp. 277–80.

69
The White Lady of Samlesbury

This famous local legend of blighted lovers is attached to the charming 700-year-old Samlesbury Hall near Preston, the administrative capital of Lancashire. The events supposedly happened in the late sixteenth century but I can find no account of the legend before the mid-1800s. However, it is at this time that the Hall was taken over by the last private owners, the Harrison family, and restored to its former glory, so it is probable that the legend came with the renovations.

After it fell once more into decrepitude, the Hall was rescued by a charitable trust and it is now open to the public from 11 a.m. to 4.30 p.m. every day except Saturdays. The White Lady is one of several attractions it offers. Future plans include the fitting out of a 'ghost room' where visitors can encounter Lady Dorothy, a collection of monks, and some child ghosts from the era when the Hall was used as a boarding school. On the day I visited, staff were preparing to do an overnight ghost vigil in the Hall for charity.

Midway between Blackburn and Preston, on a broad and rich plain of glacial drift, stands the famous old Hall of Samlesbury. The view towards the south comprehends the wooded heights of Hoghton; – on the east the background is filled in by the elevated ridges which run through Mellor, Ramsgreave, and Billington to Pendle; – the west is occupied by Preston and the broad estuary of the Ribble, the ancient Belisama; – and on the north the correctly-named Longridge leads on to the heights of Bowland; – thus enclosing a landscape which, for picturesque beauty, and historic interest, has few equals in the country.

It was here, in the early part of the reign of Henry II, that Gospatric de Samlesbury was seated in his ancestral home; surrounded by rich pastures and shut in by primeval forests of oak, from which the massive timbers were selected which formed the framework of the magnificent structure erected during the reign of Edward III [...]

Sir John Southworth [owner of the Hall in the latter half of the sixteenth century] was the most distinguished personage of his race ... but he was illiterate, bigoted, and self-willed. His rigid devotion to the [Catholic] faith of his ancestors led him to speak rashly of the changes introduced into the national religion; he also acted unwisely in contravening the laws, for which he was ultimately cast into prison, and otherwise treated with much severity until his death in 1595.

Tradition states that during his later years one of his daughters had formed an intimate acquaintance with the heir of a neighbouring knightly house [a Protestant family]. The attachment was mutual, and nothing was wanting to complete their happiness except the consent of the lady's father. Sir John was thereupon consulted; but the tale of their devoted attachment only served to increase his rage, and he dismissed the supplicants with the most bitter denunciations. 'No daughter of his should ever be united to the son of a family which had deserted its ancestral faith,' and he forbade the youth his presence for ever. Difficulty, however, only served to increase the ardour of the devoted lovers; and after many secret interviews among the wooded slopes of the Ribble, an elopement was agreed upon, in the hope that time would bring her father's pardon. The day and place were unfortunately overheard by one of the lady's brothers, who was hiding in a thicket close by, and he determined to prevent what he considered to be his sister's disgrace.

On the evening agreed upon both parties met at the hour appointed; and as the young knight moved away with his betrothed, her brother rushed from his hiding place, and slew both him and two friends by whom he was accompanied. The bodies were secretly buried within the precincts of the domestic chapel at the Hall; and Lady Dorothy was sent abroad to a convent where she was kept under strict surveillance. Her mind at last gave way – the name of her murdered lover was ever on her lips, and she died a raving maniac. Some years ago three human skeletons were found near the walls of the Hall, and popular opinion has connected them with the tradition. The legend also states that on certain clear, still evenings a lady in white can be seen passing along the gallery and the corridors, and then from the Hall into the grounds: that she there meets a handsome knight who receives her on his bended knees, and he then accompanies her along the walks. On arriving at a certain spot, most probably the lover's grave, both the phantoms stand still, and, as they seem to utter soft wailings of despair, they embrace each other, and then their forms rise slowly from the earth and melt away into the clear blue of the surrounding sky.

– Harland and Wilkinson, *Legends and Traditions of Lancashire*, pp. 261–64.

70
The Wish Hounds

This story of the phantom hounds of Dartmoor is one of a selection of traditional tales of the supernatural published in the revue The Athenaeum *in the mid-nineteenth century.*

Wish Hounds may or may be not the same as the 'Dandy Dogs' of South Cornwall (opinion differs); other names for these packs of spectral dogs are 'Yell Hounds' or 'Yeth Hounds', in which guise, according to eminent folklorist, Katharine Briggs (1898–1980), they 'pursue the demon Tregeagle' on Bodmin Moor.

The Wish Hounds, as they are called ... are under the immediate guidance of that mysterious being whose nature *Well may I guess, yet dare not tell.*

In the pauses of the storm, and mingling with the hoarse voices of the rapidly swelling mountain waters, the broken cry of dogs, the shouting of the hunters, the loud blasts of their horns, and the sound of 'hoofs thick beating on the hollow hill', are borne onward upon the winds of the forest; and when the dark curtain of mist rolls slowly up over the hill side, they may sometimes be seen to sweep across the moors, rough, swarthy, and of huge size, with fiery sparks shooting from their eyes and nostrils. It is not safe to leave the door of the house ajar; for in this case they have the power of entering, and have been known to devour sleeping children in the absence of the household [...]

Certain spots on Dartmoor are more commonly haunted by the Wish Hounds than others; and on its borders there are many long narrow lanes, closely overgrown with thorn and hazel, through which they pass in long procession on particular nights – of which, St John's Eve is one. A person who was passing at night over the moors above Withecombe, heard them sweep through the valley below him with a great cry and shouting; and when he reached the highest point of the hill, he saw them pass by, with the 'Master' behind, – a dark, gigantic figure, carrying a long hunting pole at his back, and with a horn slung round his neck. When they reached the ancient earthwork of Hembury Fort, – which rises on a high wooded hill above the Dart, – the Master blew a great blast upon his horn, and the whole company sank into the earth.

Their appearance, however, is by no means without danger to the beholder: and even the sound of their distant cry among the hills is a forewarning of evil to those who hear it. Not long since, a number of men, with dogs and ferrets, proceeded (on the Sabbath day) to trespass on a large rabbit-warren, near the source of the water of Avon: but when they got to a wild hollow in the hillside, the dogs heard the 'Wish Hounds', and at once set up a dismal howling. They were cheered on by their masters, – but nothing could prevent them from running homewards as fast as they could; 'and at the end of a fortnight,' said the warrener, 'the dogs were all dead.'

– R. J. K. 'The Wish or Wisked Hounds of Dartmoor'.

24. *Lewtrenchard Manor, Lewdown, near Okehampton, Devon*
Madame Gould, 'The White Lady of Lewtrenchard', is supposed to walk the corridors here or be seen out in the fields sitting on a plough, her diamond rings sparkling in the frosty air. See 'The White Lady of Lewtrenchard', story no. 68.

25. *Samlesbury Hall, near Preston, Lancashire*
This lovely black-and-white country house is famed for its spectres, especially the ghost of Lady Dorothy Southworth. See 'The White Lady of Samlesbury', story no. 69.

26. *Dartmoor in January*
See 'The Wish Hounds', story no. 70.

27. *Storm brewing over the North Norfolk Coast*
See 'Black Shuck', story no. 71.

28. *Blickling Hall, near Aylsham, Norfolk*
See 'The Ghost of Anne Boleyn', story no. 73.

29. *The Old Road from Bala to Machynlleth*
It was along this road that the Revd John Jones was riding when his life was saved in mysterious circumstances. See 'The Guardian on a White Horse', story no. 75.

30. *The Ruins of Llanthony Priory, near Abergavenny, Monmouthshire*
It was from here that a Herefordshire man set out to walk over the Black Mountains to Longtown and met a helpful stranger. See 'The Guide of the Black Mountains', story no. 76.

31. *The Black Pool*
See 'The White Lady of Longnor', story no. 82.

PART 4

The Twentieth Century

Introduction

In general, twentieth-century ghost stories do not differ very radically from those of the nineteenth century. Some changes can be detected, though.

There is an increase in the number of ghosts of suicides, murdered people and accident victims, who return simply because they left life too abruptly. These ghosts tend to haunt locations rather than people and often have no particular purpose for returning – they simply cannot rest. The ghosts who walk in haunted houses are of this type, and include numerous phantom monks, nuns, and ladies of various hues. Mysterious noises may be heard, too, or phantom footsteps; rooms may suddenly get very cold; disembodied heads or hands may appear or ineradicable bloodstains stain the floor. Poltergeists continue to disturb innocent families, and the ghosts of celebrities prowl round ruined mansions.

The most notable twentieth-century change is the popularity of stories in which spectres appear to strangers and are mistaken for living people. In tales of previous centuries, ghosts or wraiths may have appeared in their own form and been mistaken for the living person, but – crucially – they appeared only to those with whom they had a special relationship. However in the nineteenth century, stories of life-like apparitions appearing to strangers started to be commonplace, and by the mid-twentieth century were one of the more popular types of ghost story. These stranger-ghosts were very often specific to a particular place or situation and offered protection for those in danger. Though, as in the past, alarming and malevolent apparitions were still thought to haunt specific locations (there are several examples in the Peacock Collection), the new motif of the helpful stranger-ghost gained ground over the older concept (see, for example, 'The Guide of the Black Mountains' and 'The Guardian on a White Horse', story no. 76 and 75).

Another new motif makes its appearance later in the century, in stories of personal experience in particular. These narratives illustrate a common modern belief that the loving souls of dead family members are somehow aware of the lives of those they left behind and can continue to provide help, guidance and protection in times of crisis. I call these 'witnesses'. Occasionally, these 'witnesses' may be seen or heard, or even smelt, around the house, but mostly they are experienced through a sense of their continuing presence. In life they were figures of power and authority (particularly husbands and mothers), or close siblings, deeply loved children, aunts and uncles, nieces and nephews, or grandparents. They constitute a sort of community of the loving dead, and their presence is seen as an extension of ordinary family life. 'A Presence', story no. 95 in the Bennett Collection is a typical example, but no. 92 '"Cut the Girth Cord, Bill!"' and no. 97 'Toshing' also rely on similar motifs and beliefs.

The selection below, which falls into three distinct parts, cannot of course show all these trends, but it aims to be as representative as possible.

Part A
Stories from Printed Sources

The first group of twentieth-century narratives are legends and personal experience stories taken from books published in the first half of the century – folklore collections, compilations of ghost stories, and works by regional writers. Though they can be found in books, the stories show evidence in terms of style and content of having been heavily influenced by the oral tradition, and will almost certainly have been told orally as well as in print.

71
Black Shuck

The 'Black Shuck' of the Fenlands is perhaps the most famous of many 'Black Dogs' – archetypical terrifying animal ghosts.

If this were a stormy night the old fisher-folk of the coast would say it were just the time for Black Shuck to be abroad; for he revels in the roaring of the waves, and loves to raise his awful voice above the howling of the Stile. Black Shuck is the 'Moddey Dhoo' of the Norfolk coast. He takes the form of a huge black dog, and prowls along dark lanes and lonesome field footpaths, where, although his howling makes the hearer's blood run cold, his footfalls make no sound. You may know him at once, should you see him, by his fiery eye; he has but one, and that, like the Cyclops, is in the middle of his head. But such an encounter might bring you the worst of luck: it is even said that to meet him is to be warned that your death will occur before the end of the year. So you will do well to shut your eyes if you hear him howling – shut them even if you are uncertain whether it is the dog fiend or the voice of the wind you hear. Scoffers at Black Shuck there have been in plenty; but now and again one of them has come home late on a dark stormy night, with terror written huge on his ashen face, and after that night he has scoffed no more.

– Dutt, *Highways and Byways of East Anglia*, p. 216.

72
The Dying Mother

This touching personal experience story was told by the novelist and poet Thomas Hardy in an interview for the Pall Mall Magazine *in 1901.*

My mother believed that she once saw an apparition. A relative of hers, who had a young child, was ill, and told my mother she thought she was dying. My mother laughed at the idea; and as a matter of fact she apparently recovered and went away to her home at some distance. Then one night – lying broad awake as she declared – my mother saw this lady enter her room and hold out the child to her imploringly. It afterward appeared (I need scarcely tell you) that she died at that very time; but the odd thing was that, while she was sinking, she continually expressed a wish that my mother should take charge of the child.

– Archer, 'Real Conversations', p. 531.

73
The Ghost of Anne Boleyn

The ghost of Anne Boleyn is said to walk in many locations including Hever Castle, Bollin Hall in Cheshire and, of course, the Tower of London. In this story she haunts the place she was born (Blickling Hall, a large and handsome red-brick mansion near Aylsham, Norfolk), riding in a phantom coach and carrying her head in her hands.

Fortunately it is beyond the power of any antiquary to banish the Blickling rustics' belief in the Blickling ghosts. These are the ghosts of Anne and her father,

Sir Thomas Boleyn. On every anniversary of her execution, Anne revisits the home of her childhood. She rides in a black hearse-like carriage drawn by four headless horses and driven by a headless coachman. She is dressed all in white; and her hands support her severed head, which rests upon her knees. Just before midnight this startling apparition appears and advances slowly up the avenue which leads to the hall. At the hall door it vanishes; but within the old Jacobean mansion there are corridors along which a headless spectre glides. No one heeds it; for the occupants of Blickling Hall have grown accustomed to its visits – even the servants hear without a tremor the rustling of its ghostly garments. But the appearance of Sir Thomas Boleyn is not to be treated with such calm indifference, Sir Thomas has a yearly penance to perform; he must cross in a night forty county bridges. He, too, rides in a coach drawn by headless horses, which have a greater incitement to speed than whip and spur; for wherever they go they are followed by a pack of horrible fiends, who, as they pursue the coach, rouse the countryside by cries as fearful and awe-inspiring as those of the old Fenland bogles, the 'hell hounds of the marshes'.

Another version of this story has been set to rhyme. It tells of how, when news of the death of Anne and her brother Lord Rochfort was brought to Blickling:

That very time, at dead of night
Four headless horses took their flight
Dragging behind them as they ran
The spectre of a headless man.

Beneath his arm his head he bore
Its tangled hair all wet with gore
Pursued he was by demons foul
With piercing shriek and dismal howl.

O'er hedge, o'er ditch, o'er fence, o'er gate
They gallop on at heedless rate.
Over twelve bridges they must bound
Ere morn shall stop their horrid sound.

Sometimes by Fastolff's ruined tower
They through the neighbouring country scour,
Their snortings loud (without their heads!)
Make people tremble in their beds.

– Dutt, *Highways and Byways of East Anglia*, pp. 207–08.

74
The Ghostly Horseman

This legend, told as a personal experience story, is quoted by J. Wentworth Day in his splendid 1954 compilation of ghost stories, Here are Ghosts and Witches *(pp. 100–01). The original, now difficult to obtain, was published in a Welsh folklore collection of 1911.*

Rhos-y-Wlad is in West Wales, near Tregaron, Ceredigion.

I was going home one evening from my work from Ros y Wlad, and had to go through Rosmerherin. That place you know is a terrible spot for its ghosts. People say that they are seen there in broad daylight. As to myself I did not see them in the daytime, but many a time was I kept there all night by Jack-a-Lanterns.

I saw a ghost in the form of a cat there also, and when I began to strike him he disappeared in a blazing fire. But now for the gentleman. I was near the spot where I had seen the cat when I heard the sound of a horse coming after me. I jumped to one side to make room for him to pass; but when he came opposite me he did not go forward a single pace faster than myself. When I went on slowly, he went slowly; when I went fast, he went fast. 'Good night,' said I at last, but no answer. Then I said it was a very fine night, but the gentleman on horseback did not seem to take any notice of what I said. Then thinking that he might be an Englishman, I said in English. 'Good night,' but he took no notice of me still.

By this time I was beginning to perspire and almost ready to fall down with fright, hoping to get rid of him, as I now perceived that he was the Devil himself appearing in the form of a gentleman. I could think from the sound of the saddle and the shining stirrups that the saddle was a new one. On we went along the dark narrow lane till we came to the turnpike road, when it became a little lighter, which gave me courage to turn my eyes to see what kind of a man he was. The horse looked like a soldier's horse, a splendid one, and his feet like the feet of a calf, without any shoes under them, and the feet of the gentleman in the stirrups were also like the feet of a calf. My courage failed me to look what his head and body were like.

On we went till we came to the cross-road. I had heard many a time that a ghost leaves everybody there. Well, to the cross-road we came. But ah! I heard the sound of the ground as if it were going to rend, and the heavens going to fall upon my head; and in this sound I lost sight of him. How he went away I know not, nor the direction he went.

– Davies, *Folklore of West and Mid-Wales*, unknown page.

75
The Guardian on a White Horse

Mary Lewes prefaces the account below with this reflection: 'Cases of apparitions that have acted as protectors in danger to the percipient are occasionally heard of, and one of the most interesting stories of this type was recorded in a well-known Welsh newspaper, about two years ago, and will quite bear repetition in these pages.' She then quotes what she says are the original words thus:

A story which appears strange even in these days of telepathic experiment has appeared recently concerning the Rev. John Jones, of Holywell, in Flintshire, one of the most prominent preachers of his day. He was once travelling alone on horseback from Bala to Machynlleth, where the country is wild and desolate. When emerging from a wood he met a man carrying a sickle. The man had been seen by the minister at an inn when passing. In answer to a question, the minister gave information as to the time by his watch, and a short time after, noticed the man had furtively moved into the field, and was running alongside the hedge, removing the straw from his sickle as he ran. Then he noticed the man trying to conceal himself behind the hedge near the gate through which Mr Jones would have to pass. Firmly believing that the man intended to murder him, the minister bent his head in prayer. As he did so the horse became impatient, and started off so suddenly that the minister had to clutch the reins, which had fallen on the neck of the steed. Turning round to see if there was any available help, the minister was astonished to find close to his side a horseman in a dark dress, mounted on a white horse. No previous sound had been given of the stranger's presence. Mr Jones told him of the danger he feared, but no reply was vouchsafed, the stranger simply looking in the direction of the gate. Then the minister saw the reaper sheathing his sickle and hurrying away. The gate was reached, the minister hastened to open it for his mysterious companion, and waited for him. But the guardian on the white horse had disappeared as silently and unobserved as he arrived.

– Lewes, *Stranger Than Fiction*, pp. 39–40.

76
The Guide of the Black Mountains

This story, very similar in theme and structure to the preceding one, comes from just the other side of the Welsh border and from approximately the same time. Here, though, the ghostly guardian is identified.

Llanthony Priory, a ruined former Augustinian foundation in the Black Mountains area of the Brecon Beacons National Park, is in the care of CADW. It is 7 miles north of Abergavenny on the old road to Hay-on-Wye, in the wild and gloomy Vale of Ewyas. From Llanthony the road rises steeply to the Gospel Pass over the mountains before dropping down into Hay.

The Priory, it is said, is on the site of a hermitage built by St David, the patron saint of Wales. Legend has it that the present building was put up by a Norman knight, William de Lacy, who came across St David's hermitage when he got lost in the Vale of Ewyas during a hunting expedition and was overcome by an urge to mend his sinful ways. From that day, the Priory guidebook explains, William never removed his armour, but whether that was as a form of penance, the writer wryly remarks, 'or due to corrosion brought about by the dank atmosphere of the valley has not been clarified'.

Longtown, a village at the foot of the mountains in the next valley, has a small ruined castle with a circular keep, and lies almost due east of Llanthony over some extremely steep and inhospitable terrain. The first part of the narrator's route may have followed what is now the Beacon's Way, a long-distance route designed for experienced walkers only.

A few years ago a man was driving a lady from Longtown to Llanveyno, and she, being a stranger, questioned him concerning the 'Apparition of our Lady' at Llanthony. He replied that he did not believe in it at all; there were indeed spirits to be seen on the mountain, but they were different. He had seen, and he knew. Once he went to see friends at Llanthony, and was returning directly over the mountain to Longtown, when a fog came on suddenly and he lost his way. He was standing, quite at a loss, when a man came towards him, wearing a large broad-brimmed hat and a cloak. He did not speak but beckoned, and the man followed him, until he found himself in the right path. Turning round, he thanked his unknown friend, but received no reply; he vanished quickly in the fog. This seemed strange, but he thought no more till, on visiting his friends at Llanthony later, they asked if he reached home in safety that evening, as they had been anxious. When the stranger in the broad-brimmed hat was described they looked at each other in surprise. 'What!' they said, 'tell us exactly what his face was like.' He described the stranger more minutely. 'It was T— H—, for sure,' they cried, 'he knew the mountain well, and *he has been dead these two years*.'

– Leather, *The Folklore of Herefordshire*, pp. 36–37.

77
'Here I Am Again!'

This story was sent to Lord Halifax, an avid collector of ghost stories, in a letter of 10 July 1917.

Dear Lord Halifax,

I send you herewith my plain, unvarnished tale, according to your kind request. I may say in confidence that the house was [in] Deal, but I would rather that my name and the name of the house should not be mentioned in case you care at any time to give publicity to the story. The only tales dealing with ghostly phenomena which seem to me to be of any value are those relating first-hand experiences. All others are so embroidered that the truth of them is merely a matter of surmise.

My experience was horrible, so much so that I have vowed never to have anything to do with spiritualism in any shape or form, I want no more materializations, which seem to be the goal of all ardent spiritualists.

The house in question is an old Georgian house in Deal. It was built about 1740 and Nelson addressed many of his letters to Lady Hamilton from there, calling it 'dear — House'. My host and I had been yachting together, and on our arrival from the sea unexpectedly found the house full of relations who had come to stay. A bed was arranged for me in a dressing-room. On a previous visit I had heard that the house was haunted and that all the daughters had seen the figure of someone they called their great-grandmother gliding about. The servants had been terrified, and in consequence of what they saw had refused to stay. I had forgotten this. I was in rude health after my Channel cruise and nothing ghostly was discussed before I retired to bed.

In the middle of the night I awoke, feeling that something uncanny was about me. Suddenly, there appeared at my bed-side the phantom of either an old man or woman, of dreadful aspect, who was bending over me. That I was wide awake is beyond all question. I at once became cataleptic, unable to move hand or foot. I could only gaze at this monstrosity, vowing mentally that if I ever recovered from this horrible experience I would never dabble in table-turning, Planchette, etc. again, for here was a real materialization and the reality was too terrifying for description.

Next morning I told my host privately of what had occurred. He said he was not in the least surprised, as everybody living in the house except himself had, at one time or another, seen something of the sort.

Twenty years passed and I had almost forgotten the incident. I had frequently re-visited the house and had seen nothing. Then one day I was again invited and found my host alone. We played billiards together and retired rather late. I was suffering from toothache and on getting into bed was utterly unable to sleep. The room was in a different part of the house from the dressing-room in which I had slept on the occasion of my first visit.

Suddenly, although it was early summer, I began to feel very cold. I seemed literally to freeze from my feet upwards, and, although I put on more clothes, the cold rapidly increased until I imagined that my heart must be failing and that this was death.

All at once a voice (unheard physically) appeared to be saying over and over again to me: 'Here I am again! Here I am again, after twenty years.' Once more, in an exact repetition of my feeling twenty years before, I was conscious of the presence of something unseen in the room. I pulled myself together and said to myself, 'This time I will see this thing through and definitely prove whether my former experience was an hallucination and whether there really is such a thing as a ghost. I am wide awake beyond all possibility of doubt and only too conscious of a raging toothache.'

The thing again spoke to me mentally: 'Look round. Look round.'

I now had that unaccountable feeling of horror which all accounts of such manifestations agree in declaring are produced on such occasions. Turning round, I saw in the corner of the room facing me a curious column of light revolving spirally like a whirlwind of dust on a windy day. It was white, and as I gazed, it slowly drew near to me.

'Here I am again!' the thing kept repeating. I stretched out my hand for the matches at my bedside. As the thing got gradually closer and closer to me, it rapidly began to take human shape. Under my eyes and within my grasp it assumed that very figure I had seen twenty years before. There was no doubt whatever about this, and having reached the limit of my endurance, I shouted out, 'Who's that?' No answer coming, I hurriedly struck a match and lit a candle.

Next morning I told my host what had befallen me. He was greatly interested, and related two weird occurrences in the house, both of which had taken place during the three weeks previous to my visit.

On the first occasion he was in his dressing-room, when a servant came up to say that a friend had called to see him. He ran hurriedly downstairs and, as he turned on the landing for the next flight, he saw the figure of a man rushing upstairs. My friend, unable to stop himself, put up his hands to avert a collision and went right through the figure.

The second occasion had been when one evening an officer of Marines came to play billiards with him and brought his dog, which lay down under the table.

Suddenly the dog sprang up and began barking furiously at something invisible in the corner. It went on barking till its mouth foamed and its hair stood on end. They endeavoured in vain to calm it. From under the table it kept making violent rushes at the corner, and then retreating again. Neither my friend nor the officer who was visiting him saw anything.

– Wood, *Lord Halifax's Ghost Book*, pp. 143–47.

78
Lady Goring's Dream

This story resembles a legend attached to Ballachulish House near Glencoe in the Scottish Highlands and recorded in Alasdair Alpin Macgregor's Ghost Book *(1955, pp. 35–36), also, of course, André Maurois's better-known short story 'La Maison'.*

One of the more unusual features of this narrative is that it relates to actual events – the trial for murder in Austria of the French-born naturalised Englishman Henry Perreau (alias Henri de Tourville) for the murder of his second wife in July 1876. The trial was extensively covered in the press, not only the local Cheshire newspaper, The Warrington Guardian, *but also the international* New York Times. *The latter, under the headline 'Murdered in the Tyrol', is available online. The reporting makes it clear that evidence about the death of de Tourville's first mother-in-law, Eliza Brigham at Foxley Hall, Lymm, Cheshire, was influential in reaching a verdict of murder.*

The article recounts the details of this first death as follows: 'On August 11, 1868 [Mrs Brigham] was killed while handling a loaded revolver which de Tourville showed her.' Suspicions that he had shot her deliberately were immediately aroused because of his known hostility towards his mother-in-law, but the Coroner's jury brought in a verdict of accidental death. Later, however, it transpired that de Tourville had discussed with a Dr Albert Glynn how he might get rid of his mother-in-law, and the details of his plan coincided with the way Mrs Brigham had actually died. All these suspicions were brought up again at the trial and it seems that it was generally accepted that he had indeed murdered his mother-in-law.

The scene of the murder and the cover-up that followed are imaginatively recreated in Lady Goring's dream. One is invited to assume that the 'old house' of her dream is 'the old manor in Cheshire' which Lord and Lady Goring considered renting. Foxley Hall was pulled down in the mid-1960s; a modern housing estate now stands on the site.

One night Lady Goring distinctly saw in a dream an old house, which was quite unfamiliar to her. She knew that someone was with her and that she was visiting this house for a purpose; and when she got inside, one special room was fixed in her mind. First, it had a very curious frieze near the ceiling; then the latticed windows were of a peculiar, long, narrow shape and were connected by a striking moulding. In her dream she saw an elderly woman sitting hunched up in an armchair by the fire: but a moment later her attention wandered from her to the door, which was softly opening. She saw a man enter, steal up quickly to the elderly woman, who was apparently asleep, suddenly produce a pistol, place it close to her temple, and fire. When his victim fell over, the murderer tried to arrange the pistol so that it might appear as if it had fallen from her hand. He then noiselessly left the room, shutting the door after him, but a few moments afterwards reappeared and made some further alterations in the position of the dead woman and the pistol. Having done so, he went away and did not return. Lady Goring saw his face so plainly in her dream that it became fixed in her memory.

In course of time she and her husband, Sir Craven, wished to rent a house, and inspected various properties, among others an old manor in Cheshire. The moment Lady Goring entered the manor she felt that the place was strangely familiar to her. Then the truth rushed upon her. 'I have never been here in my life,' she told herself, 'but it is the house of my dream.'

At that moment the caretaker said, 'This door on the right leads to the drawing-room'; whereupon Lady Goring corrected her, saying, 'I am sure you must mean the dining-room.' The caretaker apologised and replied, 'Did I say the drawing-room? I meant to say the dining-room.'

As soon as she opened the door, Lady Goring recognised the remarkable frieze, the latticed windows and the peculiar moulding. There was also a chair near the fireplace.

The caretaker, on being asked for some information about the house, told the Gorings that the last tenant had not stayed very long and that the family previously in possession had been foreigners. She thought that they were Austrians or Swiss. There were three of them, a gentleman, his wife and his mother-in-law. There had been a sad tragedy in their time because the old lady had shot herself. After this, the husband and wife had gone away to foreign parts and the house had been shut up for some time.

Lady Goring did not take the house, but some months later, as she was walking down Regent Street and idly looking in at the shop windows, she came to a standstill opposite the Stereoscopic. What had stopped her was a photograph in the window. 'Why!' she exclaimed to herself, 'there is the murderer of my dream!' On going into the shop and enquiring who the man in the photograph might be, she found that it was Tourville, who was then being tried for the murder of his second wife in the Tyrol.

– Wood, *Lord Halifax's Ghost Book*, pp. 165–67.

79
The Small Cold Hand

After briefly summarising the traditional Cornish legend of Tregeagle (see story no. 66), the compiler goes on to tell this very different and much more modern-seeming tale about a neighbouring farm.

[This farm contains] a room of which this uncanny thing is said – that if you are left alone in it by night, a small, cold hand is gently laid in yours. Nothing is heard, but, softly, confidingly, as if human warmth were what it sought, this little icy palm steals into yours, and nestles there.

– Norway, *Highways and Byways of Devon and Cornwall*, p. 339.

80
The Telephone at the Oratory

This story, though told here as personal experience, closely resembles a group of traditional legends usually referred to as 'The Ghost in Search of Help for a Dying Man'. Legends of this type have been told since at least the late nineteenth century in places as far apart as the USA and Russia. For example, a story like this swept through the Russian city of St Petersburg during December 1891. Under the headline 'A Mysterious Fact', the earliest of several newspaper reports of what they called a 'miracle' told how a priest was asked to go to a house to administer the Last Rites to a dying man. When he got there he was baffled because the young man who answered the door said he was the only person who lived there and he was perfectly healthy. The priest insisted that a young lady had approached him in the street and asked him to go to the house. To prove it, he pointed to a portrait hanging on the wall:

'This,' he said, 'is the young woman who brought me here.'

'But that's a picture of my dead mother!' said the young man.

He was so awestruck that he decided to take communion with the priest, and by the evening he was dead.

Lord Halifax, whose story from his Ghost Book *is printed here, says he was told it as the personal experience of a priest. Lord Halifax met the priest in March 1919 and persuaded him to record his story. The account is dated April 1919 and signed by the priest, who declares that 'the above narrative is correctly and truly stated'. Compare this story with 'The Country Doctor's Tale' (no. 91).*

One afternoon a short time ago I was asked to visit a lady (a Mrs P—), who was ill. The house was in Montpelier Square, and when I arrived there I was met by the doctor who begged me not to administer the last rites at that particular moment, but to be satisfied with giving the patient a few cheering words and urging her to make an effort to recover; in fact, not to give herself up. I consented, but when I saw the lady I greatly regretted my promise and the fact that the doctor should have made such a request, as I feared the patient was much worse than I had been given to understand. However, the promise had been given, so I arranged that I would come back in the morning and administer the Last Sacrament. Before I left the house, however, I gave the nurse our telephone number and asked her to ring me up if her patient should become suddenly worse.

That night, as usual, the telephone was switched on to the room of one of the Fathers, in case a sick call should come through. I went to bed at my usual time, and in the early morning was awakened out of a deep sleep by the opening of my bedroom door. By the light of the moon, shining through the uncovered window, I saw a figure standing by the door. I understood the person to say something about a sick call. I sat up in bed and said, 'Speak more clearly. I don't hear.' As I spoke I saw, as I thought, by the light of the moon, the white collar of the Father-in-Charge.

This time he spoke more clearly, 'There is no time to lose. There is a telephone message.'

The word 'telephone' brought back to me in a moment my visit of the previous afternoon. I did not, therefore, ask for the address, but sprang out of bed, the door closing as I did so. Turning on the light, I observed it was just a quarter to four. I quickly dressed and went to the Chapel, noticing on my way there that the Father who had called me had forgotten to turn on the light. Going as fast as I could across the space between the house and the gates that shut it off from the main road, I found to my surprise that the gates were locked, so that I had to knock up the lodge porter to let me out. Within a minute or two I was well on my way to the house I had visited in the afternoon.

On arrival I noticed that there were lights in the windows, and after my first ring I looked at my watch and saw that it was five minutes to four. I rang again and again and presently a clock in the neighbourhood struck the hour. Once more

I rang, thinking it strange that after they had telephoned for me no one should be there to answer the door. Still no one came, and my regrets of the previous day came upon me with redoubled force. I banged at the door, making enough noise, as it seemed to me, to waken the whole household. I could see that the electric light was on in the hall and on the staircase, and I remembered that there were only six people in the house, the sick lady in one room, her husband, who was also seriously ill, in another, and the nurses. Evidently, I thought, the two day-nurses must be asleep and the two night-nurses must be in attendance on the patients. On the other side of the road, at frequent intervals, a cat was squalling horribly.

I still waited on. It was impossible for me to go back after the telephone call, but it seemed more and more strange that I should be kept waiting in this fashion. I again rang furiously, the peals reverberating through the whole house. I looked at my watch and it was twelve minutes past four. At last I thought I would get a stone and throw it at one of the lighted windows, but just as I was about to do this, the cat again made its horrid noise and I threw the stone as hard as I could in its direction.

At that moment, the clock chimed a quarter past four and to my great relief the door opened.

I did not wait to ask any questions, but went straight up to Mrs P—'s room, where I found the nurse kneeling by the bedside saying some prayers. I noticed that she was startled as I entered and I also heard Mrs P—'s voice saying, 'I do wish Father C— would come.'

I was told afterwards that for the space of about half an hour before my arrival she had been expressing a wish to see me and that in consequence the nurse had asked if she should read some prayers. I begged the nurse to leave the room for a few minutes, heard Mrs P—'s confession, and administered the Last Sacrament.

Within an hour or two she became unconscious and, after reciting the Prayers for the Dying, I was preparing to leave the house when the nurse began to thank me for coming. 'You know, you quite startled me,' she said.

I replied: 'On the contrary, my thanks are due to you for telephoning.'

'But I did not telephone,' she answered.

'Well,' I said, 'somebody did. Perhaps it was Mrs P—'s sister.'

The next morning, on going to speak to the Father whose duty it was to answer the telephone, I said: 'I am sorry I spoke to you so sharply last night.'

'What do you mean?' he asked.

'Why,' I replied, 'when you came to call me.'

'But I never did call you last night,' he answered.

'Oh yes, you did,' I said. 'You came to my room at a quarter to four this morning and told me there was a telephone sick call.'

He answered: 'I never left my room last night. I could not get to sleep, and as it happens I know that I was awake at that very time as I had my light on. What is more,' he added, 'there was no telephone call last night.'

On enquiring at the telephone exchange I was informed that there was no record of any call to the Oratory on the night in question.

– Wood, *Lord Halifax's Ghost Book*, pp. 133–40.

81
The Wernafon Ghost

'Another incident which seems to have fore-shadowed death ... recurs to my mind,' writes Mary Lewes when introducing this account, 'and though trivial in a way, it yet possesses a certain impressiveness, perhaps from its very simplicity and lack of any dramatic element.'

The reader must imagine one of the most peaceful and beautiful spots in Wales, where there stands a large, square house called Wernafon, backed by hanging oak woods, beneath which flows a clear river. Higher up the vale the stream loiters through pleasant meadows, affording the angler many a tempting pool; but as it reaches Wernafon, it begins to sing and clatter over stone and shingle as if it already heard the calling of the not far-distant sea, while in flood-time, heavy water rushes down, deeply covering stepping-stones, and swamping shallow fords. So, for the convenience of the Wernafon workmen and labourers, and others who live on the hither side of the river, it is spanned near the house by a narrow, wooden foot-bridge, which saves people a considerable walk round.

Many years ago, there lived on the Wernafon estate, two labourers, whom we will call Ben and Tom; and these men were great friends. They had worked together from boyhood, and when at last 'both being old' Ben died, Tom felt sadly lonely and forlorn. One day, soon after his friend's funeral, he had occasion to cross the river by the little foot-bridge, and as he trudged heavily along its narrow planks, his head bent down in melancholy thought, he suddenly came to a full stop, for there was a man standing in the middle of the bridge. Moreover, as he looked hard at the man, he somehow became aware that it was Ben who stood there, and who smiled at Tom as if glad to see him. Entirely forgetting for the moment that he had seen Ben buried but a few days before, Tom accosted him, and a short conversation ensued between the two about ordinary, every-day matters. But suddenly Ben asked his friend 'if he would like to see the inside of Wernafon, for,' said he, 'I go there every night, and a strange sight it is to see the people all asleep while I pass through.' He then offered to take Tom through the house that very night, if he would meet him again on the bridge at midnight; and without waiting for an answer, he glided along the bridge, and disappeared.

Immediately and with a feeling of horror, it dawned on Tom that the man he had just talked to had actually been dead for several days, and he began to think he had seen a vision or had had some extraordinary dream. Nevertheless, being a courageous old fellow, and at the same time curious to see if any result would follow, he determined to keep the strange appointment. So midnight found him waiting on the little bridge. A bright moon illumined the river and banks, and by its soft light, the old workman was presently aware of a dark shape hastening to join him. Greeting the living man, the apparition took his former comrade by the hand, and led him to the front door of Wernafon, which, as might be expected, was closely locked and barred. But at a touch from Tom's escort, the great door opened without a sound, and the companions passed into the hall of the house. There, the silence of sleep and complete darkness reigned. Yet without a stumble, Tom found himself mounting the staircase with his ghostly guide.

Arrived on the landing, the pair stopped before a closed door, which immediately opened, allowing them to enter. Softly they crept into the room, Tom remarking that it seemed filled with a faint bluish light, unlike anything he had ever seen before. They gazed at the occupant of the room wrapped in deep slumber, and creeping out again, visited all the other rooms in turn, Tom becoming more and more bewildered by the strangeness of his experience. At last 'how he hardly knew' he found himself standing again in the moonlight outside the front door; and turning to speak to his friend, discovered that he was alone. He rubbed his eyes in astonishment, for an instant before, Ben had been standing himself in such an unusual place at so late an hour, nothing remained to show that his adventure had been real and not a dream. He went home, wondering greatly at what had happened, and it does not appear that he saw the apparition again before his death, which occurred suddenly, only a few days after his mysterious experience.

– Lewes, *Stranger Than Fiction*, pp. 34–37.

82
The White Lady of Longnor

This story was printed in an issue of a local newspaper and attributed to 'an old copy' of a local parish magazine. It seems to be an amalgamation of two familiar urban legends – 'The Vanishing Hitchhiker' and 'The Devil at the Dance'.

The White Lady of Longnor comes out of the Black Pool, and flits about the roads. She was disappointed in love, rural gossips say, and so perambulates at the old trysting time, in hope to meet her faithless swain once more.

There used to be a public house called 'The Villa' where much junketing, merrymaking, and dancing was in vogue amongst the rustics on high days and holidays.

Here there suddenly appeared amongst the pleasure party a sweet, fresh, lovesome girl, dressed all in white, as if for a festal occasion.

She danced with one swain after another, and the fun grew fast and furious till at length the more sedate members of the party began to exchange suspicious glances, and suddenly the whisper went forth, 'The White Lady of Longnor.'

The whisper had barely gone the round when the place of the strange visitor was void. She had disappeared as suddenly and unaccountably as she came. This was her wont, and the party, in compliance, broke up and dispersed.

As a labourer, who was practically a contemporary of the incident remarked, 'Theer was never no more dancin' at "The Villa".'

– Cutting from *The Buxton Advertiser*, 24 June 1933. n.p.

Part B
Stories Collected by Mabel Peacock

Mabel Peacock (1856–1920) was one of the most active regional folklore collectors of the early years of the twentieth century. In 1908, in collaboration with Mrs Eliza Gutch (1840–1931), she published Examples of Printed Folk-Lore Concerning Lincolnshire, *as a contribution to the Folklore Society's 'County Folklore' series. In the following years she expanded the material she had not used for this book and by 1920 was beginning the task of readying the whole collection for publication. She died, however, before she had completed this task. After her death, the work was taken over by her friend Wilhelmine Fowler (b. 1867). The new collection consisted of all the material that had been omitted from her book with Mrs Gutch, plus stories and traditions collected since the publication of that work. When it was completed, the typescript was lodged in the Folklore Society's Archive, where it languished until the 1960s. Subsequent attempts to get the whole volume into print were unsuccessful, but I have recently produced a shortened and edited version of Peacock's text as a CD ROM. Entitled* Mabel Peacock's Folklore and Legends of Lincolnshire, *it is available from the Folklore Society. The selection of stories printed here come from Chapter 3 of that work. They have never before been published in print.*

They were told either to Peacock herself or to Wilhelmine Fowler, by local people from many walks of life – teachers, doctors, clergymen, country landowners, agricultural labourers and household servants.

83
The Ashby Boggard

I have myself known several people who have seen startling apparitions, or heard strange sounds, judged to be connected with the spirits of the departed. Still, the majority do allow that ghost stories may originate from a misconception of ordinary events.

About the beginning of the nineteenth century Ashby, in the parish of Bottesford, had a knocking ghost of some notoriety. The following account of it was written in 1907 by a gentleman, then between seventy and eighty, who was a friend of the family:

About a hundred years ago there stood an old cottage in the village of Ashby, which had the reputation of being haunted; and many people were attracted to the place to listen to the remarkable noises heard during the night, but nothing was ever seen of this mysterious character. Amongst others, two brothers John and George H. of Manton, who feared neither man nor devil either on the earth or out of it, determined to investigate, and if possible capture, kill, or dispose of the boggard. Each man armed with a long stick, or his peg (used on the warren for netting rabbits) went to the cottage and there spent the night sitting in the parlour in the dark; for this ghost, like many other ghosts, refused to demonstrate except in the dark. About midnight, a noise was heard in the chamber above, and something invisible came down into the parlour and made a noise on the table, giving several loud raps. Now was the time for the brothers to take action with their sticks, which they did with all their strength, striking the table for some considerable time, which was repeated by the ghost. After a while the candle was lighted and the noise was distinctly heard going up the chimney. This was repeated several times during the night, but no one was ever able to account for the singular noises above stated. Whether the cottage is standing at the present time, or whether the ghost has been laid by the usual plan of levelling the haunted building with the ground, the writer is unable to say.

84
The Grayingham Waggoner

At Grayingham, Mrs T. and a companion once went to draw water from the spring in the Kealed Ash close. On the north side of the road which runs up the hill past the gate leading to the rectory, they heard a lad whistling as he came up the lane with his waggon and horses. Suddenly he broke off his tune with a cry, causing the women to drop their buckets and run to see what had happened. From what the lad said it was plain that the ghost of a waggoner, who had been crushed and killed some time before when driving this very team, had appeared and got into the waggon. The two women were so much impressed by the story they sped home without their buckets, fearing to return to the well lest they should 'meet something.' It is well-known that a ghost does appear in this lane.

85
The Gunby Lovers

The Gunby ghosts 'come again' in memory of a love tragedy. A young girl fell in love with her father's coachman, who returned the feeling. The father found out that his servant dared to so think of his daughter, and determined to rid himself of the man by shooting him as he sat on the box of the carriage. As they drove along a stretch of road obscured by trees his design was put into execution. The crack of a pistol was heard and the coachman fell from his seat. But the crime brought its own punishment. The uncontrolled horses dashed madly forwards, the carriage was overthrown, and the murderer killed. When the news was carried to the girl she ceased to eat, drink, or sleep, and wasted away. The spirits of the murdered man, and the murderer with ghostly horses and carriage, are, or only a few years ago were, still to be met with on the road where the evil deed was done.

86
The Hob-Thrust

This creature is evidently of the same race as the Scotch Brownie, and the Yorkshire Hob, or Robin-Round-Cap. His stronghold is, or was, an iron pot in a cellar at the Manor Farm [East Halton]. According to one report this pot contained sand and bones, the latter said to be children's thumb bones. If the contents of the pot were stirred, Hob-Thrust would show himself at twelve o'clock. What he was like, or what he did, I do not know. I have been told that for many years the mistress of the house was much troubled if anyone meddled with the sand and bones.

Another account of the Hob-Thrust was derived by my informant from Mrs S. the owner of the farm. Once when Mr S. had a fancy to go over the whole house, and came at last to the cellar, the wife of the bailiff, who had for some time occupied the dwelling, demurred, observing that there was a Hob-Thrust in it.

'A what?' asked Mr S.

The woman replied, 'Well sir, a kind of devil.' She explained that some years ago a family then inhabiting the house were so much annoyed by this creature that in spite of having been there for more than a century, they made up their minds to leave the old home. The household goods were already on a waggon, and they were about to start when the Hob-Thrust who was the cause of the removal, peeped out of an empty splash-churn on the load, and remarked, 'We're flitting.' On hearing these words the family saw how useless it was to try to get away from him, and settled down in the house again, where he has been ever since, living in an iron pot or cauldron.

'Well, I should like to see the pot,' said Mr S. at the end of this narrative. So he and the bailiff's wife went into the cellar, the woman locking the door behind them carefully, lest the Hob-Thrust should escape. Mr S. saw the iron pot, which appeared to be half full of sand, but the bailiff's wife would not allow him to touch it, assuring him that misfortune would follow. She declared that people said the pot had been there for two hundred years at least. Her belief was that if 'the devil' is undisturbed in his iron tenement he will do no harm; but if the pot be removed, or turned over, or even touched, bad luck of some kind will result.

87
'Maister is Gone at Last'

Several years ago there was a woman who lived in Ashby Screeds. For some nights she had been helping to nurse a sick man, who 'lived neighbour to her'. But one evening his own wife had taken her place while she went to Scunthorpe to do some shopping. On her return, and close to her own house, she had to pass up a 'smootin' [a narrow passage between two houses] and her horror may be imagined when she saw the dying man lying across the top of the passage, with glassy eyes fixed upon her. She could not reach her own door without passing him, and she dared not turn her back on him, so calling up all her courage and staring him straight in the face, she walked forward and stepped over him. When she had 'safely cleared him' she felt drawn to look back, but he had vanished.

There had not been time for him to get up, much less to leave the passage, so she felt sure that he was 'a warning'. At this moment his wife opened her door, saying, 'I thought I heard you. Maister is gone at last.'

'I knew he had,' said the woman. 'If he meets me again I shall go an' all.'

88
Pins in the Keyhole

The old court house, Kirton-in-Lindsey, was said to be haunted by the ghost of a lady who burst a blood-vessel, and died suddenly at a dance once held there. An old gentleman told me in 1907, that when he was a boy some sixty years previously, he and his companions had a theory that if you put pins into the keyhole of the entrance door, and then ran round the building nine times and afterwards peeped through the keyhole, you would see the ghost of the lady.

89
The Shag Foal

Another story [was] told in 1900 ... The subject under discussion was the sale of Bell-Hole Farm, and someone frivolously remarked that the land ought to go for a good price, as the purchase would include 'a boggart'. On this, a Mr D. remarked that he did not believe in such things himself.

Nevertheless, he did know a strange story about Bell-Hole which he did not feel able to account for. His children's nurse was at one time a Mrs W. a clever, strong minded woman, who had no belief in nonsense of this kind. She laughed at people who were foolish enough to credit it. On a certain evening, she went to see neighbouring friends, who when dusk came on, suggested to her that she had better leave them, because before she could reach home she must pass the haunted Bell-Hole. Mrs W. made answer that she did not believe in that kind of thing. Then she was asked, 'What should you do if you saw a ghost?' 'Put it in my pocket,' she replied, and after a while set off home. All went well till she reached Bell-Hole, but then a thing appeared. It was a dark colour, like a very large dog with long shaggy hair, and the ears of a horse or ass. This monster took up a position behind her, keeping just to her pace as she hurried on, the while repeating, 'You'll put me in your pocket, will you? You'll put me in your pocket, will you?' Mr D. heard Mrs W. tell the tale on many occasions, and always in a manner which showed she had the fullest conviction that she was describing what really happened.

90
'Sich a Cup o' Tea as Niver Was'

At South Ferriby, on the Humber, 'there used to be something at a house'. This something came every night till the old man and his daughter who lived there hardly dared to remain alone. The father occupied a bed that 'had rods an' curtins on rings all round it. Of a night the curtins used to fling theirsens about, an' there was sich a cup o' tea as niver was, for they used to draw themselves backwards and forwards, and twist round the old man's neck, trying to strangle him'.

One night when the daughter's 'young man' called, and was talking to her by the fireside a frightful noise began in the room overhead. The young man, who had heard of the ghost, started up and asked what was the matter. The girl tried to pass the affair off, but almost immediately a dish began jerking about, and the old man told his daughter that the ghost had ordered him to meet it alone that night, on the hill behind the church. When evening came he had not the courage to go, but sat up very late instead, shivering by the fire. When he did go to bed something got hold of him on the stairs and nearly strangled him. The next night he went to the hill, and on his return seemed much shaken and 'oversetten'. When asked what he had seen his only answer was, 'Ask me no questions – the thing will never trouble us no more.' And it never did. The old man could not be made to say what he had seen on the hill behind the church, but replied to all questions as he had done at first.

Part C
Stories from the Bennett Collection

The final group of stories come from my personal collection of ghost stories and urban legends which has been assembled over the last thirty years or so from formal interviews and informal conversations with family members, friends, neighbours, colleagues and students. The majority of the stories printed here were told by elderly women (now deceased) and recorded during informal conversations and interviews in the 1980s. Unless otherwise stated, all are reproduced in their original spoken form without changes or editing.

91
The Country Doctor's Tale

One dark night, very late, a country doctor was surprised to hear a knock at his door. When he answered it he saw a frail-looking young woman standing there. 'Come quickly,' she said. 'My father is dying!' He had never seen the girl before, but she was obviously sincere, so he grabbed his bag and followed her into the night. She took him to a remote cottage, and opened the gate for him, and he went up the path to the door. He expected that she would follow him and let him in, but when he turned to speak to her she wasn't there. He waited a while to see if she'd gone in by some back door and would come round to let him in. But nothing happened. So he knocked on the door.

A woman came to the door, in tears, very distressed.

'Oh, doctor!' she said. 'Thank God you've come. I think he's dying.' She took him upstairs to a bedroom where a man lay in bed, clearly very ill indeed. The doctor stayed with him all night and by the morning the man was out of danger. The doctor took a little breakfast with the woman then got ready to leave the house, sure the man would continue to recover now the crisis was over.

'Thank you so much,' said the woman. 'You've saved his life. I prayed you'd come but I could find no way of getting a message to you. I couldn't leave him alone.'

'Your daughter came for me,' he said, puzzled. 'Where is she? It's strange I haven't seen her all night.'

'My daughter?' the woman said. 'My daughter's dead.'

'Dead?' he said. 'But she came for me and said her father was dying.'

'She couldn't have done,' said the woman 'She's been dead three years. That's her picture on the mantelpiece.'

– This story was told in a church sermon in a village on the Welsh-English border in the early 1950s.

92
'Cut the Girth Cord, Bill!'

Dad had been dead for about three years probably. Bill was working at the time of the story for a local farmer, and he used to have to go to market with these cart horses ... and he was going to Tenbury market one terrible frosty day. It was a dark morning, early morning, and the leading horse slipped and fell.

Bill would be at this time only fifteen or sixteen at the most and no experience. He was stuck in a country lane with a horse – and the load all up like this – the one horse had dragged the other horse down. And he didn't know what to do a little bit! And he said (this is the story), you know how you do? 'Oh, help me! Help me! What shall I do? What shall I do?' and saying it out loud.

And he said Dad's voice came to him quite clearly, said, 'Cut the girth cord, Bill! Cut the girth cord!' and he cut the girth cord and the leading horse got up and he was able to go, and he got to Tenbury very shaken, very frightened, but the load intact.

– Family legend told by my mother in 1983.

93
'Father's Dead!'

A cousin of mine, she was very, very old when she died. She was very sensitive.

We knew her mother wouldn't last, she was sleeping downstairs. My cousin had gone to bed (they'd been sitting up with the mother, then she had gone to bed). And she said her father came and woke her and he said, 'Your mother wants you,' and she got up, went downstairs. And her brother was there and he said, 'What have you come for?' and she said, 'Well, my father came and said she needed me.'

He said, 'Father? Father's dead!' and she said, it was only after –

She said, 'Oh,' she said. 'He came in. I heard him cough.' And he came in, and he shook her and said, 'Your mother wants you.'

And she got up, and she said it was only when her brother said, 'Father? Father's dead!' – and he'd been dead years.

[G. B. What happened next?]

Oh, she died. She died very soon after that.

– Family legend told by 'Alma' interviewed in Manchester in February 1982.

94
A Nasty Ghost

Some people came the other night with this little boy [to view the house the narrator was selling], and he was about four, they said he was about four. And they took this child round with them, and they got as far as the fourth bedroom.

And he hadn't said very much at all, but apparently he liked the cellar – he thought that was terrific!

And then they went up to the room at the top which we've always called the attic: we no longer call it the 'attic'; we call it 'the fourth bedroom' now!

And the child came down, sat in the corner for a minute, and he told us this most fantastic story about there being a ghost up there!

I said, 'A ghost?' I said. 'I've never seen one. I'd love to see one. What's he like?'

'Oh, he's a nasty one, a nasty one.'

So his father said, 'Well, there's nice ghosts as well as nasty ones.'

'Oh, this was a nasty one, Daddy.'

I said, 'Well,' I said. 'What did he look like?'

'Oh, I didn't see him,' he said. 'I heard him. He was talking to another ghost, and he was nasty too!'

– Personal experience story told by 'Joan'
interviewed in Manchester in January 1983.

95
A Presence

I don't know whether you'd call it a superstition, but I do believe it's very close to you at times of trouble or anything.

[G. B. Some people say that their mothers particularly –]

Particularly my mother, yes, particularly my mother. I feel her presence. And I will say this. After she died, it was quite twelve months after she died before I felt that her presence was no longer in the house. I felt she was there in some form or other, and her bedroom seemed to be full of her for quite a long time, nearly twelve months afterwards. And then all of a sudden –

We went away for the – well, the second holiday afterwards – and I came back and the room was empty.

Now I've never told anyone else before, but it was very strong.

But she was with me all that long time, and then she was gone. She was gone.

– Personal experience story told by 'May'
interviewed in Manchester in February 1983.

96
The Reluctant Ghost

[G. B. Do you believe it's possible for the dead to come back at all?]

I do. I believe it. My family don't, but I do, yeah. I'll give you an idea.

Once we were in Spain on holiday to a camp for five weeks and Bill started, my husband started getting terrible headaches, and we were all swimming, and he got friendly with some Scottish people and we all went swimming and that, and Bill got one of his headaches, and he couldn't see where he was going so they helped him in, and that night I was so shocked, instead of asking God to help, which he does do, I asked my dad, and as I say I was very close to my dad, and in my dream, maybe I was dreaming, he came back but he didn't want to come back. He really looked weird, you know, he was – He didn't say anything, but he was a bit cross with me, as I thought, for bringing him back, if you know what I mean.

[G. B. And you did actually see him in this sort of dream?]

I did, yes, because he looked very unhappy, and I'd never do it again. No! Because I think once you go you're rested and that, and I think in one way you're so happy you don't want to come back. This is what I think.

So, that's the only experience I've had.

Anyway, Bill had to have an operation on his head, and he was OK afterwards, and he was in neuro-surgery for two months. He had hit the side of his head with a box and he didn't remember doing it, being greengrocers. It was inside and it bled.

– Personal experience story told by 'Winifred'
interviewed in Manchester, March 1982.

97
Toshing

[G. B. Did you ever have anything like this happen?]

Only when I was doing that house, and yet I wasn't a bit afraid of it!

[Daughter, *aside*: Bill, that was her brother who'd died, told her how to paint the house for his wife to sell.]

[G. B. What about that? What Bill told you?]

Well, like, when I was doing the cupboard, he'd say, 'Now tosh inside that corner, Rachel!'

[G. B. 'Tosh?']

Paint. That's a right old-fashioned word for 'paint'. 'Now tosh inside that corner, Rachel. Do it proper!' and yet!–

I didn't turn round to look for him, but it was his voice, and he helped me to paint that house! It's really funny. He said, 'Paint it lightly and very quickly. Paint it light and very quick, the gloss paint, not like the other, the undercoat,' and honestly, he helped me paint that house!

Well, I think he wanted to thwart my brother-in-law, because he was right nasty about it. He said, 'You won't get a b– hundred pounds for that house!' and we got £390 for our Ellie, Bill's widow like. That's a long while since, love, and I went up every night, four doors away, and I painted the lot! Kitchen and all! I did! Upstairs! Everywhere! And it looked something like when I'd finished you know, and I was really proud of it! But prouder when the money came and our Ellie had her share.

And I never told my husband. He used to say, 'There's a terrible smell of paint, Rachel,' and I said, 'Get away! You've got paint on the nerves, Arthur!' But he must have been right, because it was me, you know! I'd a pair of our Bill's old overalls and I used to put them on when I went up, and I felt he was helping me. It's true! and I could have stopped there all night.

And Arthur says, 'Where the hell have you been?'

And I said, 'I've been right over the back with the dog.'

Poor Judy! Poor Judy had never been anywhere! If only that dog could have talked, she'd have had a story to tell!

– Personal experience story told by 'Rachel'
interviewed in Oldham in September 1983.

98
The Vanishing Hitchhiker*

The teacher was talking one day about ghosts and she said that her friend had been out for the evening with a gentleman friend, and they'd spent the evening in Leeds and were driving home very late, on a very wet, dark night. And, as they were driving home, they passed a bus-stop and there was a young girl standing at the bus stop, and they drove straight past and then thought it was odd she should be standing there so late. So the young man said he would go back and see if the girl was still at the bus-stop, and if she was still there he would give her a ride home. So he went back to the bus stop and found the girl still there and asked if he could give her a ride because she was getting very wet and there were no more buses that night.

So he asked her where she lived. She gave him the address. So they set off. They'd driven a little way when he had to stop at some traffic lights – and when he looked, she'd gone – couldn't be seen! He couldn't understand it at all. Very perplexed about it.

So they decided they'd go to this address that the girl had given. Knocked at the door. An elderly lady answered it and they said, 'Does a young lady live here? – because they'd given a ride to this young lady the night before who'd given this address and couldn't find her. She'd just disappeared; they didn't know where she was.' And the old lady burst into tears and said that was her daughter who had died years earlier on that same day in an accident at those traffic lights!

**This version of familiar urban legend was told to me by a friend in the early 1980s as the true experience of a friend of her son's schoolteacher. I recorded the story and have published it elsewhere in its original form (see Bennett and Smith,* Urban Legends, *p. 290), but I have slightly tidied it up here to make it more readable.*

99
The Wife in the Attic

Now, this is a funny thing!

I married a man who had been married before, and when we came to set up our own house he had everything from the old house brought in and it had to be exactly in the same way. Nothing had to be altered, and if any china was broken, it had to be bought just the same. I didn't realise this, mind you, when I married him.

There was a big photograph of his wife – a big lithograph, really, of his wife – right over the mantelpiece, sitting in a chair, and I used to have nightmares she wasn't really dead. She was alive in the attic. We hadn't got an attic! Or she was in the basement room, which we hadn't got either, neither attic or basement!

But I had to do everything in the house as she said so, and when I went cleaning round the house, sometimes I'd knock myself against the sideboard or whatever, and I'd feel she'd knocked me against the sideboard. This was just because I had to have everything the same, you know, that's the only thing.

But to think she was alive and telling me – and that if I got knocked or trapped in the furniture, I thought she was doing it. It did affect me, as I say, always having this photograph in front of me, and having to have everything the same way. You kind of felt she was the boss, you know.

– Personal experience story told by 'Inez'
interviewed in Manchester in January 1983.

Bookend 2

100
Old Grindrod's Ghost
(Lancashire Ballad)

Old Grindrod was hanged on a gibbet high,
On the spot where the dark deed was done;
'Twas a desolate place, on the edge of a moor,
A place for the timid to shun.

Chains round his middle, and chains round his neck,
And chains round his ankles were hung:
And there in all weathers, in sunshine and rain,
Old Grindrod, the murderer, swung.

Old Grindrod had long been the banquet of crows,
Who flocked on his carcass to batten;
And the unctuous morsels that fell from their feast
Served the rank weeds beneath him to fatten!

All that's now left of him is a skeleton grim,
The stoutest to strike with dismay;
So ghastly the sight, that no urchin, at night,
Who can help it, will pass by that way.

All such as had dared, had sadly been scared,
And soon 'twas the general talk,
That the wretch in his chains, each night took the pains,
To come down from the gibbet – and walk!

The story was told to a Traveller bold,
At an inn, near the moor, by the Host;
He appeals to each guest, and its truth they attest,
But the Traveller laughs at the Ghost.

'Now, to show you,' quoth he, 'how afraid I must be,
A rump and a dozen I'll lay;
That before it strikes One, I will go forth alone,
Old Grindrod a visit to pay.

'To the gibbet I'll go, and this I will do,
As sure as I stand in my shoes;
Some address I'll devise, and if Grinny replies,
My wager, of course, I shall lose.'

'Accepted the bet; but the night it is wet,'
Quoth the Host. 'Never mind!' says the Guest;
'From darkness and rain, the adventure will gain,
To my mind an additional zest.'

Now midnight had toll'd, and the Traveller bold
Set out from the inn, all alone;
''Twas a night black as ink, and our friend 'gan to think,
That uncommonly cold it had grown.

But of nothing afraid, and by nothing delayed;
Plunging onward through bog and through wood;
Wind and rain in his face, he ne'er slackened his pace.
Till under the gibbet he stood.

Though dark as could be, yet he thought he could see
The skeleton hanging on high;
The gibbet it creaked; and the rusty chains squeaked;
And a screech-owl flew solemnly by.

The heavy rain pattered, the hollow bones clattered,
The Traveller's teeth chattered – with cold – not with fright;
The wind it blew lustily, piercingly, gustily;
Certainly not an agreeable night!

'Ho! Grindrod, old fellow!' thus loudly did bellow,
The Traveller mellow, – 'How are ye, my blade?' –
'I'm cold and I'm dreary; I'm wet and I'm weary;
But soon I'll be near ye!' the Skeleton said.

The grisly bones rattled, and with the chains battled,
The gibbet appallingly shook;
On the ground something stirr'd, but no more the man heard,
To his heels, on the instant, he took.

Over moorland he dashed, and through quagmire he plashed:
His pace never daring to slack;
Till the hostel he neared, for greatly he feared
Old Grindrod would leap on his back.

His wager he lost, and a trifle it cost;
But that which annoyed him the most,
Was to find out too late, that certain as fate,
The Landlord had acted the Ghost.

– Verse by William Harrison Ainsworth,
printed in Harland and Wilkinson,
Ballads and Songs of Lancashire,
pp. 253–56.

Sources and References

Andrews, William, ed., *Church Treasury of History, Custom, Folk-Lore, etc.*, London: William Andrews, 1898.

Anon., 'The Haunted Chamber', *The Athenaeum* (28 August 1847), 912.

Anon., *The Ordnance Survey Leisure Map of Cornwall*, Automobile Association & Ordnance Survey, revd ed., 1992.

Anon., 'Review of *Tales about Wales, with a Catechism of Welsh History by a Lady of the Principality*', *The Monthly Review, or, Literary Journal* (September–December 1837), 546–58.

Anon., 'The Story of the Great Giant of Henllys', *The Athenaeum* (28 August 1847), 911–12.

Archer, William, 'Real Conversations Recorded by William Archer: Conversation II – With Mr Thomas Hardy', *Pall Mall Magazine* (23 April 1901), 527–37.

Aubrey, John, *Miscellanies upon Various Subjects*, 1696; 4th ed., London: John Russell Smith, 1857.

Aubrey, John, *Remaines of Gentilisme and Judaisme*, 1686–87; published for the Folklore Society in London by Satchell Peyton & Co., 1881.

Baring-Gould, Revd Sabine, *Cornish Characters and Strange Events*, London: J. Lane, 1905.

Baxter, Richard, *The Certainty of the World of Spirits Fully Evinced*, 1691; repr. London: H. Howell, 1840.

Bell, Henry, *Lutheri Posthuma or Luther's Last Divine Discourses*, London: William Du-gard, 1650.

Bennett, Gillian, *Traditions of Belief*, London: Penguin, 1987.

Bennett, Gillian, ed., *Mabel Peacock's Folklore and Legends of Lincolnshire*, CD ROM, Folklore Society, 2009.

Bennett, Gillian and Paul Smith, *Urban Legends: A Collection of International Tall Tales and Terrors*, Westport and London: Greenwood Publishing, 2007.

Blakeborough, Richard, *Wit, Character, Folklore and Customs of the North Riding of Yorkshire*, London: Henry Frowde, 1898.

Bond, William (see Defoe).

Bovet, Richard, *Pandaemonium*, 1684; repr. Wakefield: E. P. Publishing/Rowman & Nicholson, 1975.

Bowker, James, *Goblin Tales of Lancashire*, London: W. Swan Sonnenschein & Co., 1883.

Briggs, Katharine M., *A Dictionary of British Folk-Tales in the English Language, part B, Folk Legends*, London: Routledge, 1971.

Briggs, Katharine M., *A Dictionary of Fairies, Hobgoblins, Brownies, Bogies and Other Supernatural Creatures*, Harmondsworth: Penguin, 1977.

Briggs, Katharine M., *The Folklore of the Cotswolds*, London: Batsford, 1974.

Burne, Charlotte Sophia, *Shropshire Folklore: A Sheaf of Gleanings from the Notebooks of Georgina Jackson*, London: Trench Trübner, 1883–86.

Campbell, Eliza Constantia, *Tales about Wales, with a Catechism of Welsh History. By a Lady of the Principality*, 2nd ed., ed. Captain Basil Hall, Edinburgh: Robert Cadell/London: Whittaker & Co., 1837.

Chambers, Robert, *The Book of Days: A Miscellany of Popular Antiquities in Connection with the Calendar*, 2 vols, Edinburgh: W. & R. Chambers, 1869.

Chambers, Robert, *The Popular Rhymes of Scotland*, London and Edinburgh: W. & R. Chambers, 1870.

Couch, Jonathan, *The History of Polperro, A Fishing Town on the South Coast of Cornwall*, 1871; condensed version, Cornish Publications, 1965.

Crowe, Mrs Catherine, *The Night-Side of Nature: Or Ghosts and Ghost-Seers*, London: Routledge, 1848.

Day, J. Wentworth, *Here Are Ghosts and Witches*, London: Rider, 1954; repr. New York: Dorset Press, 1991.

Davies, Jonathan Ceredig, *Folklore of West and Mid-Wales*, Aberystwyth: Welsh Gazette Offices, 1911.

Deane, Tony and Tony Shaw, *The Folklore of Cornwall*, London: Batsford, 1975.

Defoe, Daniel, *The History of the Life and Adventures of Mr Duncan Campbell ...* London: E. Curll, 1720 (sometimes ascribed to William Bond).

Defoe, Daniel, *A Political History of the Devil*, Durham: G. Walker, 1726.

Defoe, Daniel, *A True Relation of the Apparition of one Mrs Veal ...* , London: B. Bagg, 1706.

Dobson, William, *Rambles by the Ribble*, Preston: Dobson, 1883.

Dutt, William A., *Highways and Byways of East Anglia*, London: Macmillan & Co., 1923.

Gage, John, FRS, 'A letter from John Gage, esq FRS, Director, to Sir Henry Bell KH FRS, Secretary, accompanying a Gold British Corselet exhibited to the Society, and since purchased by the Trustees of the British Museum', Article XXII, *Archaeologia: or Miscellaneous Tracts Relating to Antiquity*, vol. 2, 1835.

Gilbert, C. S., *An Historical (and Topographical) Survey of the County of Cornwall*, 2 vols, Plymouth Dock: no publisher cited, 1817–20.

Glanvil, Joseph, *Sadducismus Triumphatus*, London: Thomas Newton, 1681.

Goldsmith, Oliver (attributed), *The Mystery Revealed: Containing a Series of Transactions and Authentic Testimonials Respecting the Supposed Cock Lane Ghost*, London: no publisher cited, 1742.

Gomme, George Laurence, ed., *English Traditions and Foreign Customs: A Classified Collection of the Chief Contents of* The Gentleman's Magazine *from 1731 to 1868*, London: Elliot Stock, 1885.

Grenville, George, Baron Nugent, *Some Memorials of* John *Hamden, His Party and his Times*, London: Chapman & Hall, 1864.

Gutch, Mrs Eliza, *Examples of Printed Folklore Concerning the North Riding of Yorkshire*, London: David Nutt for the Folklore Society, 1901.

Gutch, Mrs Eliza and Mabel Peacock, *Examples of Printed Folklore Concerning Lincolnshire*, London: The Folklore Society, 1908.

Hardwick, Charles, *Traditions, Superstitions and Folk-Lore of Lancashire*, 1872; repr. Manchester: Morten Publishers, 1973.

Hardy, Thomas, ed. Michael Millgate, *The Life and Works of Thomas Hardy*, London: Macmillan, 1984.

Harland, John and T. T. Wilkinson, *Ballads and Songs of Lancashire*, Part 2 *Modern*; repr. of 3rd ed., Wakefield: E. P. Publishing, 1976.

Harland, John and T. T. Wilkinson, *Legends and Traditions of Lancashire*, London: George Routledge and Sons/Manchester: L. C. Gent, 1873.

Hawker, Revd R. S., *Hawker's Tales of Ghosts and Witchcraft*, Penzance: Oakmagic, 1997. Originally published in *Footprints of Former Men in Far Cornwall: Selections*, London: John Lane, 1893.

Henderson, William, *Folklore of the Northern Counties*, 1866; repr. Wakefield: E. P. Publishing, 1973.

Hitchins, Forescue, ed. Samuel Drew, *The History of Cornwall, From the Earliest Records and Traditions, to the Present Time*, Helston: no publisher cited, 1824.

Hole, Christina, *Haunted England*, London: Batsford, 1940.

Holland, Richard, *Supernatural Clwyd*, Llanrwst: Gwasg Carreg Gwalch, 1989.

Hunt, Robert, *Popular Romances of the West of England; or, the Drolls, Traditions, and Superstitions of Old Cornwall*, 2 vols, London: John Camden Hotton, 1865; repr. of 3rd ed. in one vol. London: Chatto & Windus, 1923.

Ingram, John H., *The Haunted Homes and Family Traditions of Great Britain*, London: W. H. Allen, 1884.

Jessopp, Augustus, *Frivola*, London: Fisher Unwin, 1896.

Kinsley, James, ed., *The Oxford Book of Ballads*, Oxford: Clarendon Press, 1969.

Lang, Andrew, *The Book of Dreams and Ghosts*, London: Longmans, 1897.

Lang, Andrew, *Cock Lane and Common Sense*, London: Longmans, Green & Co., 1894.

Leather, Ella M., *The Folklore of Herefordshire*, Hereford: Jakeman and Carver/London: Sidgwick & Jackson, 1912.

Lee, George Frederick, *The Other World; Or, Glimpses of the Supernatural*, London: Henry S. King, 1875.

Lewes, Mary L., *Stranger Than Fiction: Being Tales From The Byways of Ghosts and Folk-Lore*, London: William Rider & Son Ltd., 1911.

M. B. C. (Margaret Butler Clough), *Scenes and Stories Little Known; Chiefly in North Wales*, Mold: Whittaker and Co/London: Pring & Price, 1861.

Macgregor, Alasdair Alpin, *The Ghost Book: Strange Hauntings in Britain*, London: Robert Hale, 1955.

Morton, Andrew (alias of Daniel Defoe), *Secrets of the Invisible World Disclos'd*, London: J. Clarke *et al.*, 1729.

Norway, Arthur H., *Highways and Byways of Devon and Cornwall*, London: Macmillan & Co., 1922.

Penwarne, John, *Contemplation, A Poem; With Tales and Other Poetical Compositions*, London: Longmans *et al*, 1807.

Peters, Rod, 'Boggart Hole Clough & the 1896 Campaign for Free Speech', extract from 1984 MA thesis, *Boggart Hole Clough and the ILP, May–August 1896*. http://boggartholeclough.files.wordspress.com/2008/03/boggart-hole-clough-the-1896-campaign-for-free-speech.pdf.

R. J. K., 'The Wish or Wisked Hounds of Dartmoor', *The Athenaeum* (27 March 1847), 334–35.

Rees, Revd R. Wilkins, 'Ghost-Layers and Ghost-Laying', in William Andrews, ed., *Church Treasury of History, Custom, Folk-Lore, etc.*, London: William Andrews, 1898, pp. 241–68.

Richardson, M. A., *The Local Historian's Table Book of Remarkable Occurrences, Traditions, Legendary and Descriptive Ballads, Connected with the Counties of Newcastle-upon-Tyne, Northumberland and Durham*, London: J. R. Smith, 1843–46.

Roby, John, *Traditions of Lancashire*, 6th ed., Manchester and London: John Heywood, 1900.

Scott, Sir Walter, 'The Trial of Duncan Terig, alias Clerk, and Alexander Bain Macdonald for the Murder of Arthur Davies, Sergeant in General Guise's Regiment of Foot, June MDCC.LIV.' <http://www.readbooksonline.net/readOnLine/5165>

Sinclair, George, *Satan's Invisible World Discovered*, 1685; Gainsville, Florida: Scholars' Facsimiles and Reprints, 1969.

Smith, Martin, *Stamford Myths and Legends*, Stamford: Paul Watkins, 1998.

Thiselton-Dyer, T. F., *The Ghost World*, London: Ward & Downey, 1898.

Thoms, William J., 'The Laying of the Ghost', *Folk-Lore Record* 2 (1879), 176–77.

Underwood, Peter, *Ghosts of Wales*, Swansea: Christopher Davies, 1978.

Walton, Izaak, *The Lives of Dr John Donne, Sir Henry Wotton, Mr Richard Hooker, Mr George Herbert*, 1670; London: J. M. Dent, 1898.

Westwood, Jennifer and Jacqueline Simpson, *The Lore of the Land: A Guide to England's Legends from Spring-Heeled Jack to the Witches of Warboys*, London: Penguin, 2005.

'The White Lady of Longnor', *The Buxton Advertiser* (24 June 1933).

Wood, Charles Lindley, Viscount Halifax, *Lord Halifax's Ghost Book*, London: Geoffrey Bles, 1936; repr. London: Bellew, 1989.

List of Story Titles

Madam Pigott
'Maister is Gone at Last'
The Man in the Library
The Man-Monkey
The Master Builder's Tale
The Murder of Mr Perceval
The Murder of Mary Barwick
The Murder of Sergeant Davies
A Nasty Ghost
'Oh, Dear Son, Thee Art Dead!'
Old Coles
Old Grindrod's Ghost
Old Nanny's Ghost
Old Sykes's Wife
Padfoot
Parson Dodge and the Spectral Coach
The Phantom Battle of Edgehill
Pins in the Keyhole
A Presence
The Red Barn
The Roaring Bull of Bagbury
The Reluctant Ghost
The Shag Foal
Short-Hoggers of Whittinghame
'Sich a Cup o' Tea as Niver Was'
Silky of Black Heddon
The Small Cold Hand
A Spectral Funeral
St Mary's Place, Stamford
Stripped
The Telephone at the Oratory
Tommy and the Ghost
Toshing
Tregeagle
The Unquiet Grave
The Vanishing Hitchhhiker
A Very Dangerous Rabbit
The Wernafon Ghost
'Weep! Weep! Weep!'
The White Lady of Lewtrenchard
The White Lady of Longnor
The White Lady of Samlesbury
The Wife in the Attic
The Wish Hounds
The Wraith of John Donne's Wife
The Wraith of Mary Goffe
The Wraith of Mr Mohun
The Wynyard Wraith
'You Say True. You Are in the Right'

Index of Locations